CREATING YOUR MEDICARE RECIPE

Your guide to enrolling
on time and without penalties

Marcia MacDonald Mantell

This is an educational and informational book about the various parts and pieces of Medicare. It is intended as a guide to help those entering Medicare at age 65 or older understand the various parts, when to enroll in them to avoid penalties, and importantly, how to budget for the high cost of healthcare in retirement. Use this book as one source of information in your Medicare research. Your personal Medicare options may be different from those presented here.

Marcia MacDonald Mantell © 2024

All rights reserved. No part of this book may be used or reproduced, stored in or introduced into a retrieval system, recorded, or transmitted in any form or by any means (electronic, mechanical, photocopying, recording or otherwise) without prior written permission and consent of Marcia Mantell. Journalists or reporters may quote brief passages with accreditation for a review to be printed in a magazine, newspaper, or digital media without permission.

This book is sold subject to the condition that it shall not, by way of trade or otherwise, be lent, resold, hired out, or otherwise circulated without Marcia Mantell's prior consent in any form of binding or cover other than which it is published and without a similar condition including this condition being imposed on the subsequent purchaser.

Mantell Retirement Consulting, Inc. and Marcia Mantell are not affiliated with the federal government's Medicare program, the Centers for Medicare and Medicaid Services (CMS), or Social Security. Readers should contact Social Security for information about their specific Medicare options and current pricing. Readers should also do their own research to find the best options for their health insurance coverage. Use Medicare.gov and the "find plans" tool available at no charge.

The information presented in this book is currently available as of November 2024. It is for your general education and is not to be construed as personal financial advice. It is up to each individual to consult with their financial and tax advisors and the insurance companies they choose to work with before making Medicare decisions.

Mantell Retirement Consulting, Inc., Plymouth, MA

Cover and book design by Geralyn Miller Design.

Dedication

To three important men in my life

My dear friend, William G. Perry (1959-2022), who lost his valiant battle with cancer. He was the challenger of all parts of Medicare. I'll always remember how delighted he was to get his Medicare card. He was only on Medicare for three days before he passed. My heart still aches.

My brother, John MacDonald II. He's the only guy I know who started Medicare planning in his 50s. I so enjoy the urgent text messages he sends me with questions about Part B pricing and expected inflation on the various parts of Medicare. Keep the questions coming!

And to my husband, Daniel Mantell, who supports my rants and raves about the US healthcare system and the Medicare mess. He patiently waits while I scream every time I hear "Medicare for All." No one knows what they are talking about with that phrase. I love you best.

Introduction

I'm willing to bet if I asked you if you wanted to spend the next couple of hours learning about Medicare or if you'd rather do just about anything else on the planet, you'd choose the latter. So would I. In fact, I'd really like to be in my kitchen right now baking chocolate chip cookies.

But the fact of the matter is, I've spent the last fifteen years researching the ins and outs of Medicare. You'll only have a few weeks to figure this out. Medicare and Social Security are two key ingredients of The Social Security Act—the law the governs both federal programs. Who knew?

The Medicare law is incredibly fascinating. And insanely frustrating. It is filled with technical jargon. There are parts, pieces, and penalties. The process to get into Medicare is nothing short of nuts. Then, enter the insurance companies, the hospital systems, doctors, outpatient service providers, and nurses. Add in drug manufacturers, drug insurers, pharmacies, and PBMs (pharmacy benefits managers). There are actuaries, hedge fund managers, and lawyers also deeply involved. And the cherry on top of this Medicare sundae is none other than our Congress.

What's missing from this crazy collection of rules and regulations? Perhaps that's not the right question. We should be asking, "Who's missing from all of this Medicare mayhem?" It's us. We, the people. The American retiree who thought after 40 to 50 years of working, building a career, raising a family, and making their community better would be afforded a simple, clear, comprehensive health insurance program that supported their aging bodies, minds, and needs. Oh, how could we have been so wrong?

Medicare was somewhat easier and more affordable at the outset. But that is not what is happening today. The layers and layers of complexity resemble a 10-tier wedding cake. All the tiers are a different size, a different flavor, and have different decorations. But this Medicare cake sure doesn't taste so good.

I thought about calling this book "Medicare's Mystery & Mayhem." Or "The Medicare Mess." But those names, while true, won't really help you. I have become a consumer advocate for those making the transition into retirement. I spend a lot of time and energy helping wonderful, regular, hard-working Americans run the gauntlet to claim Social Security at the best time for them. Then watch them glaze over as they slog their way through the layers of Medicare muck.

However crazy the system is, it is the one we have today. Like it. Hate it. Frankly, it just doesn't matter. We have Medicare the law, the system, the confusion. We're not going to meaningfully fix any of it in our lifetimes. So, we better figure out now how to use it correctly. Because it only gets more and more complex as we get older.

Here's how this book might help you with Medicare:

- Provide you with some basics about the Medicare law and why it works the way it does.
- Explain the various parts and pieces of Medicare you will need for comprehensive and complete health insurance for your older years. Medicare is not just one thing.
- Show you how to figure out how much your health insurance is going to cost you. And how to plan for future costs.

- And make sure you can build a checklist so you enroll in each of the pieces of Medicare on time. This way you avoid a gap in health insurance coverage and any penalties for arriving late to this party.

Look at it as creating your own recipe for Medicare. That's essentially what each of us has to do. It really is like making a batch of chocolate chip cookies:

- We have to shop for and pay for all the ingredients we'll need. The basics (flour, sugar, butter, eggs) and the extras (chocolate chips, vanilla, walnuts, raisins). Yes on the raisins! They are my secret ingredient. Just don't ask my kids to weigh in on that.
- Measure each different ingredient in the right amount.
- Add the basic ingredients to the mixing bowl in a specific order and stir to combine.
- Then, add in the extras that make these cookies your own.
- That's how we'll tackle this Medicare maze. It's a matter of knowing the right ingredients, taking the right steps in order, and setting the temperature correctly.

Keep in mind as you read this book that you may have different options with your health insurance in retirement. The general rules are included here, but there is a lot of nuance at the individual level, and you may have different options.

Let's get started with our baking project. Set the timer. You'll be 65 before you know it!

Table of Contents

Dedication I

Introduction III

SECTION 1:
Background, Key Ingredients, & Sticker Shock 1

1 What Is This Thing Called "Medicare?" 3
    Some Medicare background 3
    Read the directions 5
    Transitioning from employer group health
    insurance to Medicare 6
    There's no home-economics class for Medicare 8
    An impossible ask of us mere mortals 9
    Making the big move to Medicare, ready or not 10

2 "Parts" and "Medicare" Aren't What You Think 11
    Medicare is not one single insurance plan 12
    "Part" is a technical term 13
    When a part of Medicare is only a "policy"
    or a "plan" 13
    Another new "Part" of Medicare is
    introduced: Part C 14
    Consumers choose what goes in their grocery cart 15
    Enter the modern miracles of medicine:
    prescription drugs 16
    The Medicare Modernization Act of 2003 creates
    Medicare Part D 17

3   It Costs How Much?! Prepare for
    Sticker Shock at the Register 19
    Your Medicare recipe has a different basket
    of ingredients 20
    Tracking healthcare costs in America 23
    Part A deductibles provide some insight 24
    Part B premiums give us another look
    at what's going on 24
    What about drug cost inflation? 25
    How much will my "Medicare" groceries cost? 27
    The importance of Social Security's COLA 30

4   Tales from Real Retirees 33
    A few tales from my work with individuals
    entering Medicare 33

SECTION 2:
Grocery Shopping For Parts, Pieces, &
Filling Your Grocery Bag 39

5   Medicare Part A—The Butter & Sugar 41
    Universal health insurance 41
    Combining the butter and the sugar 42
    FICA taxes cover both Social Security and
    Medicare Part A 43
    Part A is not the same as Part B 44
    Medicare Part A is premium-free, not free-free 45
    Skilled Nursing also comes with usage costs 46
    Other Part A coverage: hospice care 47
    Paying your Part A usage costs 47

6   Medicare Part B—Time to Add the Flour 49
    How Part B works 49
    Part B is definitely not free-free or premium-free ... 50
    You are getting a subsidy for your use
    of the medical system 52

Table of Contents

Meet IRMAA 53
Determining your Part B premium 54
Your Part B premium can change every year 55
Your Social Security payments are automatically
reduced for Part B premiums 56
What if you don't agree with the determination? 56

7 **Medicare Part D—Adding the Eggs** 59
Does your current health insurance plan offer
"creditable" coverage? 59
Part D plans are generally inexpensive, but IRMAA
applies here too 60
Shop for the cheapest Part D plan 61
Not all Part D plans cover all your drugs 62
Note the pharmacies 62
Two examples with eye-popping results 63
Can your 95 year-old parent really deal
with this mess? 65
Arm yourself for your future years 67
Do you even need to bother with a Part D plan? 68
But I have a Medicare Advantage Plan.
Do I need a separate Part D plan? 68
Can I use drug discount cards with my Part D plan? ... 69
Part D notes 70

8 **Optional Ingredient that Isn't Really
Optional—Medigap** 71
The Original Medicare supplemental plans: Medigap ... 71
How Medigap plans work 72
Medigap plans: categories of covered benefits 73
When to enroll in a Medigap plan 76
Your one and only one Medigap open enrollment,
no questions asked opportunity 76
Guaranteed Issue – buying a Medigap plan later 77

9 A Substitute to Your Medicare Recipe—
   Medicare Part C Plans 79
   Medicare Advantage is not the same as
   Medicare or Medigap 79
   The insurance company has a seat at the table...............80
   Who's paying your doctors?..81
   MAPDs gain traction..81
   A look under the hood of Medicare Advantage Plans 82
   MAPD HMO or PPO or PFFS? 83
   Two MAPD examples...84
   Top 10 questions to ask before choosing a MAPD..........87

SECTION 3:
Start Baking Earlier Than You Think—
When To Enroll In Each Part Of Medicare....................91

10 When, Where, and How to Sign Up
    for Medicare Part A and Part B 93
    Automatic enrollment vs. proactive enrollment..............93
    The Initial Enrollment Period—your IEP 94
    Hold on, we're not done with the proactive
    enrollment rules… 95
    What's with these overly complicated instructions? 96
    Baby Boomers didn't want to retire at 65 97
    Working after 65 and your health insurance 98
    Worker, 65+, enrolled in a large group health plan,
    no Social Security yet...99
    Worker, 65+, enrolled in a large group health plan,
    claimed Social Security 100
    Worker, 65+, enrolled in a small employer
    health plan, no Social Security yet 101
    Medicare Part A's inconvenient "6-month"
    retroactive period is really 9-months............................101
    Fixing HSA excess contributions 102
    The Part B SEP: Special Enrollment Period 103

Table of Contents

    The Part B General Enrollment Period 104

    Special notes for married couples and partners 106

    Where and how to enroll in Medicare
    Part A and Part B 107

**11 When, How, and Where to Sign Up for
Medicare Part D or a MAPD 111**

    Signing up for Medicare Part D the first time 111

    Contact the Part D insurance company directly 112

    Choosing a Medicare Advantage plan
    with drug coverage 113

    The Part D penalty 114

    Reshopping during annual Open Enrollment Period 115

    If you want to later switch to a MAPD or
    change your plan 115

    High degree of plan management 116

**12 Ingredients That Do Not Belong in
Your Medicare Recipe 117**

    COBRA and "Retiree" insurance are really
    for younger folks 117

    Other insurance pays secondary to Medicare
    Parts A and B 118

    The ACA Marketplace plans don't work after 65 119

**SECTION 4:
Checking Your Pantry For More—Optional
Ingredients, Important Information, Resources 121**

**13 Dental, Vision, Hearing Coverage—
Do You Really Need Them? 123**

    What happened in Congress in 1965? 123

    Finding coverage for dental 124

    Dental coverage is quite limited—
    plan for out-of-pocket expenses 125

    Vision plans are not what you may think 125

What about coverage for hearing tests and
hearing aids?..126

Can you continue employer coverage in retirement?....127

Last thoughts..128

14 Important Information for Creating Your Medicare Recipe... 129

When to get started exploring this "Medicare" thing......129

How should you evaluate your options?.......................131

Evaluating Medigap plans 132

Evaluating standalone Part D plans 133

Evaluating Medicare Advantage with drug plans..........134

Should spouses buy the same plan
at the same insurer?..137

Can't I switch from MAPD to Medigap like the
commercials indicate?...137

15 Where to Get Expert Help....................................... 141

Every state has S.H.I.P. representatives 141

Find an independent, unbiased fee-only person...........142

If you use a broker or agent, what should
you ask them?...142

Top 13 questions to ask a broker or agent –
a baker's dozen 143

16 Resources and a Worksheet to Create Your Medicare Recipe... 147

Pulling together your Medicare recipe..........................147

A Medicare and retirement healthcare cost example....148

A blank template for you to create your Medicare
recipe and estimated costs..150

Medicare resources and more 152

Endnotes... 154

SECTION 1:

BACKGROUND, KEY INGREDIENTS, & STICKER SHOCK

CREATING YOUR MEDICARE RECIPE

CHAPTER 1

What Is This Thing Called "Medicare?"

Let's start back at the beginning with a bit of history. A history of chocolate chip cookies.

The all-American favorite cookie is the chocolate chip cookie. And like most great American stories, it happened by accident. In 1938, it was not always easy to get Baker's chocolate to make desserts. Chef and restaurant owner, Ruth Wakefield, needed a dessert to serve at her popular restaurant, The Toll House Inn, located in the small town of Whitman, Massachusetts. One day she found she had run out of Baker's chocolate (supply chain issues are not new). So, she took a bar of Nestle's semi-sweet chocolate, cut it into small chunks, and added it to her basic cookie dough. Served warm, these cookies were an instant hit with the patrons.

Some Medicare background
At the same time Ruth was baking batches of Toll House chocolate chip cookies in Whitman, the Congress was working on amendments to the Social Security Act in Washington DC. This new law would provide a small social safety net for American workers when they retired at age 65 and their spouses. The original law passed in 1935 but left out provisions for widows. When a husband died, payments stopped.

In the 1939 Social Security Amendments[1], that was remedied so widows and dependent children could receive benefits.

By 1945, another discussion was percolating among members of Congress. President Harry S. Truman had proposed a national healthcare plan for the country. There were five key pillars to his plan[2]:

- Find ways to address the lack of healthcare professionals across all communities.
- Increase and grow public health services for all age groups.
- Increase funding for both medical education and research.
- Lower costs individuals had to pay for their own and their family's healthcare.
- Offer alternatives that address the loss of income to a family when a member gets severely ill.

Like Social Security, this healthcare program was not intended to be welfare or a handout. Americans would have to pay to play. Through the accumulation of funds via taxes or fees, Americans would earn "chits" toward the healthcare costs they would inevitably need in retirement.

As you might imagine, there were strong feelings among Congress members. The bill did not pass in 1946. And the next 20 years featured debate after debate of how to address rising costs and other problems within the healthcare system. It took two full decades before then President Lyndon Johnson signed the Medicare Act of 1965 into law.

To implement the new Medicare law quickly and efficiently, it was integrated into the Social Security law. The operations and mechanisms were already in place with the Social Security Administration to set up and collect incoming payments that would fund the program.

What Is This Thing Called "Medicare?"

Since its beginning in 1965, the Medicare law has been changing and adapting to modern American medical advancements and the needs of our oldest citizens.

Read the directions
It's important to note the Medicare law itself is thousands of pages long. As an older consumer of healthcare, you are the one who needs to understand the original recipe. Otherwise, everything about Medicare seems crazy. While you may never read the law books, there are three important parts of the law you should know:

1. **Medicare was never designed or intended to be free or to pay your full costs of using the healthcare system.** Most individuals paid out-of-pocket for their healthcare, or employers or unions provided insurance. But as the number of retirees rose—from 3 million in 1900 to 9.6 million by 1965 to nearly 18 million in 2023—healthcare costs continued to increase year after year. Regular Americans couldn't afford to pay for their care. When the federal government stepped in and passed the Medicare law, it found ways to share payments between individuals and general tax revenues.

2. **Workers would contribute to the Medicare system via payroll taxes.** Using the same mechanism as Social Security, a worker would contribute a percentage of wages into the Medicare system. This is part of their FICA tax. Employers also contribute a required amount on behalf of each worker. FICA is the Federal Insurance Contributions Act. Employers are required to send each worker's share to the Medicare Trust Fund, called "HI" or Hospitalization Insurance, in each payroll cycle.

3. **No one really knows how much healthcare costs.** The steps to figure out how much healthcare costs is nothing short of wildly complicated. How much do doctors

charge for their services? How does that rate get set? Can one hospital charge a different amount for the same procedure than another hospital 25 miles away? If you need a particular drug to cure a problem, can it cost more at one pharmacy vs. another?

The inside workings of the U.S. healthcare system are mostly mysterious and opaque. It is incredibly complex. There has been, currently is, and always will be two very different sides of the coin. We the people need affordable, high-quality healthcare and quick access to care when we fall ill. On the other side of the coin, we need to recognize the system itself is a business and one that needs to remain highly profitable. Can the two sides really coexist?

That's a burning question no one can really answer.

Policymakers, politicians, private lobby groups, and presidents haven't been able to simplify the system. Insurance companies, drug manufacturers, pharmacies, researchers, and consulting firms all have different perspectives and ideas. Nothing works for everyone. But everyone needs to read directions, ask questions, and navigate the complex system to find their best option for coverage.

Transitioning from employer group health insurance to Medicare

As you start the journey into Medicare, you may find it is fraught with challenges. Most folks have not been involved with their employer health insurance, so they have no grounding in health insurance. Rather, they've simply checked a box each fall during the annual enrollment period and magically have health insurance coverage come January.

That is all about to end. Critically, you need to think about health insurance as the "before age 65" era and the "at and after age 65" era. The two eras are virtually 100% different.

While covered by employer group health plans before 65, your employer reminds you to make an election for the plan in October or November. The new plan and costs start on January 1st. After 65, it's up to you to know what to do. You'll need to sign up during your Initial Enrollment Period. Or, you need to know you are eligible for a Special Enrollment Period. Medicare does not start each year on January 1st unless you have a January birthday. Except a January 1st birthday.

Get any of this wrong and you'll face permanent penalties. Or choose a plan that doesn't work for you.

When you have coverage through a group plan with your employer, you can usually cover your family—spouse, partner, minor children, disabled children of any age, young adult kids up to age 26. Once you reach Medicare, it's all individual. You only cover yourself. Everyone else is on their own.

Your employer determines your premium cost and takes it out of your paycheck. In Medicare, Social Security determines your premium, then it's docked from your Social Security check. If you want full coverage, it's up to you to find your own supplemental insurance. You choose the private insurer, the plan, and pay that insurance company.

Your prescription drug coverage was decided by your employer when you had a group plan. The premium was usually wrapped in your health insurance premium. While in Medicare you'll need to sign up for separate prescription drug coverage and pay premiums out of your checkbook to another insurer.

With employer plans, you may have options to choose additional health benefits such as dental and vision plans. If you want dental or vision coverage while in Medicare, those are separate decisions and individual payments you take on.

Or you may choose a packaged Medicare Advantage plan where you pay copays and coinsurance most times you use the healthcare system.

Employers have been creative in offering tax-advantaged accounts such as FSAs and HSAs. You can choose to participate or not in these plans and you manage them. Once you're in Medicare, no contributions are allowed into HSAs and FSAs may have different funding rules. You'll have to figure out which Medicare costs are "qualified."

When you're working, the cost of insurance is shared between you and your employer, with the employer picking up the lion's share of costs. You usually only see your share of the monthly premium—typically 15% - 30% of the total cost. Once you're in Medicare, costs are split between you and the federal government. You will pay a minimum of 25% of the total premium assessed for the year. But, if you have high income in retirement, you'll pay a much larger share of the premium.

Are you shaking your head at this point wondering what on earth all of that means? Just keep reading and you'll learn more about the "after 65" era in no time.

This overview is meant to give you a big heads up that you are entering new territory. What you've known as health insurance for the past 40 years has virtually nothing to do with Medicare. You aren't just crossing a state line on your travels. You are going to need planes, trains, boats, and automobiles to get to your new destination: Medicare. Buckle up!

There's no home-economics class for Medicare

Do you remember home-economics class in high school? You would have learned to make chocolate chip cookies in that class. And many other cooking basics like macaroni and cheese and how to cook a chicken. You would have learned about budgeting for groceries and why mashed potatoes come out better with a ricer than a mixer. All basic and essential skills and knowledge for the home chef.

What class did you take about how insurance laws work? Or about understanding how to appeal a denied claim? How about a class about how the heck you're going to afford basic health insurance when you're young, when you're covering a family, and when you're older and in Medicare?

Yeah, me neither. None of that is taught in school or college. I'd guess that 99% of employees have absolutely no idea how their employer insurance works for them. Rather, they get an email in October or November, right as the holidays are getting underway, letting them know it's "annual enrollment time." You have two weeks to select your health insurance and other benefits for the next year. Choose from behind door number one, door number two, or maybe you even have a door number three. You probably select door number one. Most employees probably think that's the best.

If you have options called gold, silver, and bronze, you probably choose gold because it must be the best. After all, it's got the gold medal.

An impossible ask of us mere mortals
And you couldn't be more wrong. Health insurance doesn't work that way. Getting the "best deal" depends on many factors about your usage of the healthcare system, whether you are covering someone with a critical or chronic illness, or if you have children on the plan. It depends on how much out-of-pocket you can afford vs. monthly premiums. It takes more than 10 minutes to figure out the best option for you and your dependents. Oh yes, how sick you will be next year? Or will you be in an accident? What if your wife will be diagnosed with breast cancer? Or your husband finds out he needs prostate surgery?

More simply put, the mere act of choosing a health insurance plan is nearly impossible. Some would say a ridiculous endeavor. And yet, that's what every American adult is expected to do. With no background, no way to really get the information, and no crystal ball. Maybe the "Magic 8-Ball" from the 1970's would work better when selecting health insurance?

By now, you probably have several employers in your rearview mirror and decades of selecting health insurance plans. You've seen changes over the decades. From the original plans where you paid no premium and only $25 per doctor visit or hospitalization. How we miss the 1980s! Then, we started paying premiums, maybe $50 per month for a family. Still $25 at the doctor's. Next came higher premiums, but no copays at the doctors, but some cost-sharing for hospitalizations. And, in 2008, the new-fangled high-deductible health plans were introduced, followed by the Affordable Care Act Marketplace in 2010.

We're used to employer-sponsored health insurance. But now, you're moving into Medicare land.

Making the big move to Medicare, ready or not
It's like you're moving from your pretty, newly renovated kitchen with granite countertops and a copper farm sink to an industrial kitchen in the bowels of a church basement. It's ten times bigger than your kitchen at home and is set up for preparing meals for hundreds at a sitting. The industrial ranges and refrigerators are from 1964. The linoleum-covered floor is scrubbed clean, but it is ancient and worn.

That's what the transition is going to be like as you move from employer-sponsored health insurance, or the ACA Marketplace, to Medicare. It's old, worn, and not very pretty. But it is reliable. You'll just need to prepare for the initial shock and the aftershocks.

CHAPTER 2

"Parts" and "Medicare" Aren't What You Think

We all use short-hand language. It's much faster to communicate.

Think about those chocolate chip cookies. The original recipe probably called for two cups of bleached flour, sifted. Today, we'd see that ingredient as 2c flour. Chefs and family cooks know exactly what that means. We learned the shorthand in the kitchen from mom, grandma, or dad.

Two trickier abbreviations easy to confuse are *tsp* and *Tbs* (or sometimes Tbsp). The first is short for teaspoon, the latter for tablespoon. There is a huge difference if you mix these up. There are three teaspoons in a tablespoon.

And don't even think about substituting baking soda for baking powder. Chocolate chip cookies call for baking soda. It is not at all the same ingredient as baking powder. Both are produced from soda bicarbonate but baking powder has an added acidic agent needed when making cakes, pancakes, and biscuits. Not these cookies. Instead, you need baking soda to improve the bake and brown the cookies.

So, understanding shortcuts and similar sounding ingredients is a basic skill set in the kitchen. It's also a needed new-found skill when it comes to "Medicare."

Medicare is not one single insurance plan
We all talk about Medicare like it's one thing. Similar to how we refer to the health insurance we get from our work. "I have Blue Cross insurance." Or "My new employer's health insurance is through Aetna." So, it's a natural assumption to say, "I'm almost 65, time to sign up for Medicare." As if it's a click of a button or a single form to sign. If only.

Medicare is shorthand for a whole host of health insurance components. Looking at it as a consumer, "Medicare" is our health insurance for our retirement years. From a hospital's perspective, Medicare means working with the federal government by way of the Centers for Medicare and Medicaid Services (CMS) for rules, regulations, and payment arrangements. From a physician's point of reference, Medicare sets the prices they can charge when accepting "assignment" and agree to take on Medicare patients.

From your perspective, Medicare is THE health insurance for older Americans and lawful residents who are 65 and older. It is also the insurance provided to people of any age if they have been diagnosed with a disability by the Social Security Administration (SSA) and are receiving SSDI—Social Security Disability Insurance. After 24 months receiving SSDI, that person's Medicare becomes automatic. It's also the health insurance for anyone with ALS or end-stage-renal disease.

Easy to mix up, Medicare is not Medicaid. These two terms are often used interchangeably but are very different. Baking soda vs. baking powder. Medicaid is the state-run, federally supported health insurance for people of all ages who meet a specific definition of low income. Each state determines who qualifies for Medicaid based on their state laws. Most states qualify individuals and families based on some income-to-poverty ratio. Both Medicare and Medicaid provide health insurance to individuals, but the programs, eligibility, and coverage are vastly different.

"Parts" and "Medicare" Aren't What You Think

Once a low-income person on Medicaid reaches age 65, they generally must enroll in Medicare. There is a special program for those on Medicare who also need Medicaid.

"Part" is a technical term

Medicare is also the umbrella term for a number of parts. There are four named parts specifically laid out in the Medicare law. You'll likely need additional insurance plans to be fully insured once on "Medicare." It is quite like shopping for all your chocolate chip ingredients and putting them in a grocery bag.

A brief review of the original Parts A and B:

- **Part A is hospitalization insurance.** It covers your care in the hospital as an "admitted patient," plus skilled nursing care, and hospice care.

- **Part B is physician and outpatient services insurance.** This part of Medicare pays your doctors and most other health professionals and specialists, and for outpatient treatments and durable medical equipment.

These two parts of Medicare are often referred to as "Original Medicare." When the Medicare Act was signed into law in 1965, only these two parts made up Medicare.

When a part of Medicare is only a "policy" or a "plan"

Neither Part A nor Part B, however, covers 100% of your costs. Again, they were designed to *help* older Americans pay their healthcare costs. To fill the gap, consumers had two choices.

1. They could pay their share out-of-pocket. However, paying out-of-pocket did not protect them from the risk of extremely high costs when they required hospitalization after a heart attack, a stroke, or another major surgery. And it did not cover them for the high costs of cancer treatments or other chronic illnesses requiring outpatient drug therapies.

2. They could buy commercial insurance. Once Medicare became the primary insurer for millions of older Americans, insurance companies built products that covered the out-of-pocket costs a senior was responsible for.

Working with CMS, insurance companies created private plans to supplement Part A and Part B—essentially to sit underneath A and B to catch all the crumbs. When seniors added a supplemental option to their "Medicare," insurance would cover their exposed costs via a separate policy. These supplemental plans are not a "Part" of Medicare. However, the ability to offer supplemental plans is laid out in the law. They are an optional piece for those on Medicare to obtain comprehensive insurance coverage. Like walnuts in your chocolate chip cookies. Some people add them. Others think that is a terrible idea. Either way, it's an option.

Each insurer must conform to the rules and regulations set out by CMS, but they have a lot of flexibility in how they price their policies.

These plans are called "Medigap" plans or gap policies. Or go by "Med Sups," shorthand for Medicare Supplemental policies. While you are not required to buy a Medigap plan, without one you are on the hook to pay your share of the costs incurred when you're in the hospital, in skilled nursing care, seeing a healthcare professional, or receiving outpatient treatments.

Another new "Part" of Medicare is introduced: Part C

Fast forward to the 1990s. Healthcare prices were on the rise, again. Medicare was costing the federal government more than anticipated. Congress was unhappy about the bite Medicare payments were taking out of the general tax revenue. Older Americans were frustrated with rising costs and couldn't afford to pay for necessary services and treatments. And commercial insurers saw a new business opportunity to provide insurance plans to large pools of older Americans.

"Parts" and "Medicare" Aren't What You Think

Insurers had developed a health insurance product that showed promise lowering costs and improving health outcomes—Health Maintenance Organizations (HMOs). This new structure of receiving healthcare included medical experts plus insurance oversight of costs. Insurers, working with CMS, tested the HMO model of healthcare with people on Medicare with promising results. Medicare +Choice was approved for seniors.

Billed as an option to get the federal government out of your healthcare (for consumers) and better able to manage rising costs (for the federal government), this substitute to Original Medicare was added to the Medicare law as Part C.

Consumers choose what goes in their grocery cart

The idea was older consumers would now have a choice. They could opt to get Medicare through a private insurance company or directly thru the government. As a bonus, they would get coordinated care in a Part C plan as they were required to have a primary care physician, or PCP, act as their "healthcare quarterback." Costs would be lower as well. All services were local, available, and favorably priced as part of a network. Plus the PCP oversaw each patient's care, reducing duplication or unnecessary treatments.

Remember, this is happening before electronic medical records. There had been no way to coordinate care, to ensure that drugs prescribed by a cardiologist didn't react with drugs prescribed by another specialist or practitioner. Medicare's primary goal from the outset was to help pay for hospitalizations and costs incurred *after* one got sick. This idea of focusing on prevention and coordination *before* getting sick should, ideally, be a model that would indeed bring the cost of healthcare down.

From the start, insurance companies offering Part C plans were paid directly by Medicare. For each senior enrolled in a private plan, Medicare paid the insurer a per-capita payment each month. Seniors with Medicare +Choice paid small copays when using the healthcare network. And, to sweeten the offer, these plans added some dental and vision cost benefits. Plus, they had options to pay for prescription drugs, all as part of coordinated care. Parts A and B of the Medicare law were written to specifically exclude coverage for these items.

Today, thanks to the never-ending ads on TV, these plans are known as Medicare Advantage plans. While these plans had such high hopes, two critical factors are left out of the advertising:

- Before you can buy a Medicare Advantage plan, you must first enroll in Medicare Part A and Medicare Part B. And you must pay your Part B premium and any Income-Related Monthly Adjustment Amounts (IRMAA).
- You will pay a share for almost every service you use in the insurers network. It might be a small copayment of $15 or $25 or $40. Or it could be a percent of the charge, say 40% of the cost for an x-ray. You pay the assigned amounts throughout the year until you reach an out-of-pocket (OOP) maximum. In 2024, that OOP maximum was $8,850 for in-network services and over $13,300 if using in- and out-of-network services. In 2025, the OOP maximum jumped to $9,350 in-network and $14,000 in- and out-of-network.[3]

Enter the modern miracles of medicine: prescription drugs
In the original design of the law, Medicare did not cover prescription drugs prescribed by a doctor and delivered at a pharmacy. It paid for drugs delivered when one was admitted as an in-patient to a hospital for surgery under Medicare Part A. Or, if receiving infusions, such as chemotherapy, in an out-patient arrangement, Medicare Part B covered those drugs.

Older Americans with chronic conditions were on their own to pay for prescriptions or over-the-counter remedies available at the time. Retirees had few options for dealing with chronic health conditions such as arthritis, cancer, coronary heart disease, and diabetes.

A new field of biotechnology was cutting its teeth in medical research in the 1970s, 1980s, and 1990s. Amazing research in various areas of medicine resulted in tremendous drug development, advancement, and manufacturing.

Seemingly overnight, health issues that plagued older Americans now had a cure, or at least a way to be managed. Lipitor (1985) was life saving for those with high cholesterol. A calcium channel-blocker drug, Verapamil (1981), was the first of a chain of drugs to manage high blood pressure. And what we see advertised as Celebrex got its start in 1993. It is a powerful drug that helps people with severe osteoarthritis and acute pain.

These drugs grew in popularity among aging Americans. They were readily prescribed to those who benefited tremendously. But as demand grew, costs for prescription meds kept rising. And rising fast.

Older people in need of these new drug marvels couldn't afford them.

The Medicare Modernization Act of 2003 creates Medicare Part D

Congress was well aware of this increasingly dire situation among the seniors they represented. But it took until the early 2000's to get serious about addressing the rapidly rising, and unaffordable, prescription drug situation. After some 20 years of kicking the can down the road, Congress was pressured to address the relentless cries about unaffordable prescription drugs for seniors.

In usual fashion, the debates were long, drawn out, and heated. It took several senators and house representatives to cross the aisle to secure funding to lower drug costs for seniors. In the end, no one in Congress was really happy. But there was a new bi-partisan law on the books.

On December 8, 2003, the Medicare Prescription Drug, Improvement, and Modernization Act of 2003 (MMA) was signed by then President George W. Bush. Standalone Medicare Part D plans became available for the first time in 2006.

In the twenty years since the MMA became law, some seniors benefited greatly. Many generic prescriptions for managing chronic illness cost only a dollar per month or less. Many other prescriptions cost less than $25 per month. Yet millions of seniors still cannot afford the more expensive or "designer" drugs with fancy names that you see advertised daily. Highly specialized drugs can cost anywhere from $2,000 per year to nearly $100,000 per year. Even if you have the money to pay for such a treatment, it's an insane amount of money. How is it some life-saving drugs cost as much as a house does in many parts of the country?

More on Part D plans and the convoluted, crazy, confusing pricing we have forced our seniors into dealing with coming up in a later chapter.

CHAPTER 3

It Costs How Much?! Prepare for Sticker Shock at the Register

Inflation is an economic principle most of us are familiar with. As someone getting close to Medicare age, you recognized the wild inflation in the early 2020's. It sure looked a lot like the 1970s and 1980s. You know how costs for most items only get more expensive over time.

Even the cost of the ingredients for chocolate chip cookies can set you back a few pennies. On my shopping trip on August 24, 2024, here's the tab for the ingredients needed for one batch of cookies:

    Chocolate chips, 1 bag, 12 ounces = $5.39
    5 lb. bag flour = $5.59
    1 lb. butter, unsalted = $7.79
    4 lb. bag sugar = $3.79
    32 oz. box dark brown sugar = $2.99
    Vanilla, 1 oz. bottle = $4.49
    1 dozen eggs, large = $4.49
    Baking Soda = $1.19
    Salt = $2.99
    Walnuts, 12 oz. shelled = $7.49
    Raisins, 20 oz. box = $4.69

That's a grand total of $50.89! Even though I understand inflation and know costs rise every year, it's still a stark reality that life is expensive. Especially if you have a sweet tooth.

Your Medicare recipe has a different basket of ingredients
One of the most frustrating realities of entering Medicare is that it is not ready to eat. Rather, you'll find you need a grocery bag to fill with multiple parts and pieces. But not necessarily all in one trip to the store.

You need all the primary ingredients to be fully and completely covered by health insurance throughout retirement. There are other cost-sharing coverage options available as well.

The four primary ingredients in a complete Medicare insurance plan are:

1. **Medicare Part A[4]**. This covers your hospitalization charges when you are admitted into a hospital. This coverage might be for a health shock (heart attack, stroke, serious fall, etc.), for a surgery (knee replacement, heart valve replacement, etc.), or an illness or accident. In addition, Part A covers skilled nursing rehab stays after a 3-day stay in the hospital. It also covers some home-health services after a surgery, and hospice.

    a. You pay "usage costs" when you are admitted to the hospital or need skilled nursing care.

    b. In 2025, your deductible when admitted to a hospital is $1,676. If you stay longer than 60 days, you also pay a daily room rate of $419. Costs increase after 90 days.

    c. And after 20 days in skilled nursing, you pay $209.50 per day, up to day 100. Then 100% of costs.

2. **Medicare Part B[5]**. Under this part of Medicare, your doctors, specialists, and other healthcare professionals get paid. Even if you are admitted to a hospital, the docs get paid under Part B. This part also covers certain drugs administered in a clinic such as chemothera-

py drugs or osteoporosis injectable drugs . If you need durable medical equipment (crutches, wheelchair, hospital bed, etc.) coverage comes under Part B. And certain home health aides that perform specific services.
   a. Your share of the costs charged for any Part B services is 20%. Part B pays 80%.
   b. You also pay the first dollars of expenditures each year. In 2025, that Part B deductible is $257.00.
3. **Medigap or "Med Supp" plans**[6]. This ingredient is an additional insurance you buy from a private insurance company. Depending on the specific plan you buy, it can cover your out-of-pocket expenses that you are responsible for under Medicare Part A and Part B.
   a. The monthly premiums range from around $60/month to more than $400/month per person. Your exact price depends on where you live and how many benefits you want the insurance plan to cover.
   b. The average price for the top Medigap plan is about $200/month per person in many areas of the country.
4. **Medicare Part D**[7]. This ingredient is specific to helping folks pay for their prescription drugs.
   a. You'll pay a monthly premium to the insurance company you've selected. The average basic premium in 2025 is about $36 per month. But if you only take tier 1 generic drugs, your premium may be much less.
   b. You'll pay the first $590 of your share of drug costs as the deductible in 2025, up from $545 in 2024. Or less, depending on your specific plan. You might pay $0 for generic drugs. Or maybe $1 or $2 per month.

c. If you reach the deductible, you'll then pay generally 25% of the cost of your prescriptions, until you reach a specific dollar cap.

We'll dive into the details of each of these Parts and plans the next sections. For now, it's important to understand you'll have 4 main ingredients to get started with Medicare.

You may add optional insurance plans for coverage the Medicare law specifically disallows in your grocery bag. Most people moving into Medicare are surprised to find out that Medicare doesn't provide insurance for:

- Dental visits, cleanings and x-rays, crowns, root canals, etc.
- Vision care including routine eye exams, glaucoma testing, eyeglasses or contacts, etc.
- Podiatry care except for diabetic routine checkups.
- Hearing aids, testing, and services.
- Transportation to and from appointments, tests, and surgeries, etc.

Each person moving into Medicare will need to decide if they want help with costs for these services. It's often less expensive to just pay-as-you-go.

Interestingly, the coverage you've been receiving for last 40 years from your employer for these services was not insurance. Rather, these are cost-sharing plans that set limits on how much they will spend on you each year. It's the same general model when you're in Medicare.

To add further fun to this grocery game, you have another choice for getting your Medicare health insurance—**Medicare Part C**[8].

This is an alternative way to buy your Medicare coverage. Another name for Part C is "Medicare Advantage." This is a type of bundled insurance whereby you enroll in Medicare Part A and Part B, but then assign your benefits over to the insurance company you've selected. You get the same coverage as in Part A and Part B, but you pay for these services in a different way.

Part C plans also bundle your prescription drugs, so it's imperative you find a plan that covers all your prescriptions. You may also find some cost-sharing or discounted extra "goodies" at different price points. And you are typically limited to a specific network your providers and facilities must participate in.

- Often, you can find a Part C plan with $0 monthly premiums…
- …but you'll pay copayments or a percentage of the services you receive nearly every time you use the healthcare system. In 2024, the in-network out-of-pocket cap is $8,850 and $13,300 for in- and out-of-network services.

Again, there's more to come in later chapters.

Tracking healthcare costs in America

Regardless of what you choose for your Medicare coverage, it's not all sugar and spice. I am acutely concerned about the never-ending escalating costs in the healthcare sector. Focusing on just three primary piece-parts of Medicare (Part A, Part B, Part D), costs have risen significantly over the decades.

However, it is challenging to find reliable data points. Nearly two decades ago, it was noted that healthcare costs rise faster than general inflation. But where are the data showing which healthcare expenditures are rising? Is there one pocket that is a problem area? Or several? Is this a problem for those under 65 or over 65?

The healthcare and health insurance systems operate in a completely opaque environment. Certain broad healthcare costs are tracked by the Bureau of Labor Statistics in their monthly watchlist of hundreds of products and services. But that doesn't help those on Medicare try to budget for their cash outlay every month and every year. For 20 to 30 years.

Part A deductibles provide some insight
Each person is responsible for some payment to cover their hospitalization charges. This is the Part A deductible. Looking at the increases in the individual's Part A deductible over time gives us an insightful look into hospital cost inflation as we age.[9]

Table 1. Part A deductible for selected years.

Year	Inpatient Hospital Deductible	% change over 10-year ranges
1970	$52	--
1980	$180	246%
1990	$592	229%
2000	$776	31%
2010	$1,100	42%
2020	$1,408	28%
2025	$1,676	19% (since 2020)

You see a dramatic increase in the individual's cost in the early decades of Medicare. Since 2000, the annual deductible has not risen as dramatically. However, average general inflation between 2010 and 2020 was about 2% per year. Yet Part A deductibles rose between 2% and 5% per year.

Part B premiums give us another look at what's going on
From a consumer view, we have a way to track certain buckets of healthcare inflation for those on Medicare. That is to see what has happened with Part B premiums over the decades. Here we see quite a fascinating story emerge[10].

Table 2. Part B base (standard) premiums for selected years since inception.

Year	Part B Monthly Premium	% Increase: over 10-year ranges
1966	$3.00	--
1976	$7.20	140%
1986	$15.50	115%
1996	$42.50	174%
2006	$88.50	108%
2016	$121.80	38%
2025	$185.00	52%

Again, Part B covers the majority of expenses for physicians and healthcare professional services, outpatient services, durable medical equipment, and some types of home health aides. The monthly premiums in Table 2 are for each person in Medicare Part B for years since Medicare began. You see in 1966, those with Medicare Part B paid $3.00 per month toward their insurance. Ten years later, the premium had increased 140% to $7.20 per month. And so on.

As of 2025, the dollar amount those on Medicare Part B pay is high—$185.00—but interestingly, the overall increases have moderated somewhat in the last two decades.

What about drug cost inflation?
Oh, the cost of drugs. This is one hot topic in America today. The recent 2022 Inflation Reduction Act certainly highlights some of the good, the bad, and the ugly of drug manufacturing, price sharing, and insurance coverage hoopla that goes on behind the scenes.

Many would say the drug manufacturers and big pharma have run amok. And they are a big piece of rising drug costs. But the health insurance industry shares some blame as they cherry pick which drugs to cover each year. And Congress should step up to take the heat on allowing drug companies to run rampant with their pricing until now.

Some of that free-wheeling at the expense of older Americans is finally coming to a head. There is a small but mighty step ahead in the latest law. It allows Medicare to negotiate with manufactures of the most costly Part D drugs. Prior to the Inflation Reduction Act, the law did not allow Medicare to negotiate prices.

Immediately and already in effect is the $35 cap on insulin and insulin products (as of 2024). That is a gigantic win. But only if you're on Medicare. And only if your preferred Part D plan covers the specific insulin you take.

In the scraps that lie on the cutting room floor from the Inflation Reduction Act are those who are not on Medicare. For younger folks, there is no cap on their insulin products, and they will continue to pay whatever the drug manufacturers set as the price.

However, in an interesting turn of events, the three major manufacturers of insulin proactively announced they would lower the cost of insulin to $35/month to include everyone not on Medicare. We'll see where this goes.

But, back to drug inflation…it's anyone's guess. Like ice cream and chocolate, there are a million reasons why prices can increase each year. The difference is we really can live without chocolate, hard as that may be. But many older Americans cannot live without the drug protocol they are on.

There is another significant effort underway to curb drug costs within the pages of the Inflation Reduction Act: all Medicare

It Costs How Much?! Prepare for Sticker Shock at the Register

beneficiaries will have a $2,000 per year cap on OOP costs for their covered prescriptions. This OOP cap begins January 2025. Furthermore, seniors' expenses can be paid in equal amounts each month. Previously, the first few months of the year have been wildly expensive. Then, costs drop significantly only to restart at the highest levels the following January.

How much will my "Medicare" groceries cost?
Let's look at a few examples how you might plan for some key costs of your healthcare throughout retirement. Since so much can and will change, let's estimate premiums and sample prescription drug costs for the next five years assuming the following for costs and inflation:

- Part A premium is $0 per month unless you or your spouse or qualifying ex-spouse did not earn 40 Social Security credits. We'll assume $0 per month.

- Part B premiums have increased an average of 5% per year over the last 20 years. Some years had big, dramatic hikes; other years price increases were more moderate. For planning, we'll use a straight line increase of 5% per year.

- Part D premiums are based on national averages for the basic premium and for the basic plus supplemental premiums. This model assumes a 6% increase in premiums each year. Your own Part D premiums may be significantly different from these estimates.

- Part D drug costs are a wild card. We'll use a low-use drug case, a medium-use drug case, and a high-use drug case. Here's where you'll see the impact of capping all OOP spending at $2,000 per year if you happen to be among the 5 million retirees needing very expensive drugs.

- These cost models do not assume surcharges in Part B or Part D that high-income people in retirement will pay. More on the Income-Related Monthly Adjustment Amounts in later chapters.

- These costs do not estimate your share of costs for services you receive. For example, no Part A deductibles are included. No 20% cost-share to see your doctor under Part B. And no allocation for supplemental Medigap premiums or for Medicare Advantage plan costs. You'll find lots of information later in the book on those ingredients.

Low-use of prescription drugs. Assume a person uses only one generic prescription drug. Here's how they might budget for the next five years.

Table 3. Budget estimates through 2028 for selected Medicare costs—low prescription use.

Low-use of prescriptions in retirement	2023	2024	2025	2026 Est	2027 Est	2028 Est
Part A Premium	$0.00	$0.00	$0.00	$0.00	$0.00	$0.00
Part B Premium	$164.90	$174.70	$185.00	$194.25	$203.96	$214.16
Part D Basic Avg Premium	$32.09	$34.50	$36.57	$38.76	$41.09	$43.56
Est Cost of Drugs	$12.00	$12.00	$12.00	$12.00	$12.00	$12.00
Monthly Total Estimate	$209	$221	$233	$245	$257	$270
Annual Total Estimate	$2,508	$2,654	$2,802	$2,940	$3,085	$3,237

This model assumes a generic drug cost of $1.00. Many Tier 1 generics cost $0 to $3 per month in 2025. You can see that by 2028, their annual budget could increase by $435. By 2039, just 13 years into retirement and continuing with the same assumptions, their annual budget will be double the amount spent in 2025.

Medium-use of prescription drugs. Now let's look at a person who takes one or more prescriptions that totaled $1,000 in 2024. This person would be considered a medium-user of Rx's. Continuing the same inflation factors and assumptions, you can see that with the estimated increases in drug costs, their budget increases at a much faster clip.

Table 4. Budget estimates through 2028 for selected Medicare costs—medium prescription use.

Medium-use of prescriptions in retirement	2023	2024	2025	2026 Est	2027 Est	2028 Est
Part A Premium	$0.00	$0.00	$0.00	$0.00	$0.00	$0.00
Part B Premium	$164.90	$174.70	$185.00	$194.25	$203.96	$214.16
Part D Basic Avg Premium	$32.09	$34.50	$36.57	$38.76	$41.09	$43.56
Est Cost of Drugs	$83.33	$83.33	$88.33	$93.63	$99.25	$105.21
Monthly Total Estimate	$280	$292	$310	$327	$344	$363
Annual Total Estimate	$3,364	$3,510	$3,719	$3,920	$4,132	$4,355

They will need to plan for an additional $636 in their 2028 budget. And their costs will double to nearly $7,400 in 2038.

High-use of prescription drugs. The most significant budget situation is for people who take high-cost drugs. Before 2024, someone in a high-cost drug situation could pay well more than $10,000 per year just for their prescriptions. In this high-use example, assume a $10,000 OOP cost for prescriptions in 2023. Look what happens as the Inflation Reduction Act takes effect, first in 2024 by limiting some OOP, and then in 2025 by capping drug costs at $2,000.

Table 5. Budget estimates through 2028 for selected Medicare costs—high prescription use.

High-use of prescriptions in retirement	2023	2024	2025	2026 est	2027 est	2028 est
Part A Premium	$0.00	$0.00	$0.00	$0.00	$0.00	$0.00
Part B Premium	$164.90	$174.70	$185.00	$194.25	$203.96	$214.16
Part D Basic + Supplemental Avg Premium	$56.49	$55.50	$58.83	$62.36	$66.10	$70.07
Est Cost of Drugs	$833.33	$291.67	$166.67	$175.00	$183.75	$192.94
Monthly Total estimate	$1,055	$522	$410	$432	$454	$477
Annual Total Estimate	$12,657	$6,262	$4,926	$5,179	$5,446	$5,726

This person won't pay over $12,000 again until 2043, 20 years into retirement. The OOP cap will increase each year for inflation, but having a cap in place is very good news for many seniors to significantly reduce their costs.

The importance of Social Security's COLA

Because prices on everything rise over the long term, you'll need some way to offset these increases when you're no longer working. Your investments should be on track to cover the lion's share of the increases due to inflation. So, you'll likely find you should be invested for growth throughout retirement. It's generally a good idea to work with a professional financial advisor who focuses on investing in retirement to make sure your assets help keep up with inflation.

Social Security has a built-in cost-of-living adjustment, the COLA. Almost every year as costs increase, your Social Security payments will also increase. While we tend to focus on the initial amounts we'll receive from Social Security, an important component is benefits increase almost every year. These increases help you keep pace with rising costs as you age.

You won't get rich with your Social Security, but at least you won't be stuck with payment amounts from 20 years ago.

CREATING YOUR MEDICARE RECIPE

CHAPTER 4

Tales from Real Retirees

Perhaps the biggest shock when leaving an employer's group plan and transitioning to Medicare is learning that Medicare is not a family plan. You cannot cover your spouse, your partner, your disabled adult children, your pets, your granny. Medicare is specific about the magic number that opens the gate. It's when you personally reach age 65. Not when your spouse reaches 65. You. Individually.

A close second is how expensive Medicare is. Most people have believed, and even budgeted, for much lower healthcare costs once they reach Medicare. In fact, many budget zero dollars. So it is a nasty surprise to learn they will indeed be paying for Medicare. Remember the earlier point about reading directions? Medicare has always been a cost-sharing situation. It has never been free.

The number one comment I hear from people who are just learning about Medicare is that they feel stupid. They've built careers, are plenty smart, but this whole program just defeats them. They aren't stupid. The problem is the insane complexity of the Medicare system.

A few tales from my work with individuals entering Medicare
Without giving you the benefit of knowing more details about what "Medicare" really means today, let me first share several tales from clients I have worked with. Helping them navigate the gauntlet is no DIY project.

The why and when and who thought this program was a good idea will unfold in the following sections about each part of Medicare. You will need to consider all the ingredients before making your own critical decisions.

Let's meet some real retirees and see where they've gotten tripped up:

- "Chris" decided to take an early retirement package from his corporate job at age 66. He assumed he'd start Medicare and cover himself and his wife "Jenny," who is only 60. That can't happen. Instead, Jenny would go on COBRA for up to 36 months, then be on her own for health insurance. He was not at all delighted about this. But Medicare has never been available for family coverage. It is based solely on each individual reaching age 65.

- "Patty" was turning 65 and retiring from one company. She was planning to take a few months off and then look for part-time work at another company. She wanted to wait to join Medicare to see if a part-time gig would offer her benefits. With taking time off and no specific prospect for a job on the horizon, this was not an option. Older Americans simply cannot be without health insurance. If you have gaps in continuous coverage, you may be hit with permanent penalties when you eventually do join parts of Medicare. Reluctantly, she agreed to sign up for Medicare.

- "Stan" retired from his company and needed to get into Medicare by September 1st. He was on track to go through all the steps. Then, his employer called and asked him to return until the end of the year. He returned but didn't restart his employer-sponsored health insurance. He also dropped the ball signing up for Medicare. When he fell and broke his arm, requiring surgery, he had no health insurance in place and had to pay several thousand dollars for using the healthcare system. Full responsibility for getting into and maintaining Medicare falls to each individual.

- Fortunately, "Samantha" called me at age 64 and 10 months. She was not going to retire for a few more years and wanted to confirm she would be fine staying on her employer's group plan. Her employer only has nine employees. No, it is not fine to stay on the employer plan. Sam had to enroll in both Medicare Parts A and B before her 65th birthday month to make sure she would be fully and completely covered. Otherwise, she would have been responsible for 80% for all Part B healthcare services she needed and most costs if she landed in the hospital. Small employers have different rules for how their insurance pays for employees who age 65 and older.

- In talking to "Justine" who retired at 64 from a large company and was on COBRA, I found out her birthday is on the first day of December. She thought she would need to get into Medicare but could wait until COBRA ran out when she was 65 ½. Nope. Not how it works. And, in fact, her Medicare would not start on December 1st, the month of her 65th birthday. It will actually start on November 1st. If your birthday falls on the first of any month, your Medicare start date is the month prior.

- "Henry" had been working since he was 18 years old. He's now 84 and is ready to retire. He's never enrolled in Medicare Part B because he's always had health insurance from a large employer. He was sure he was going to be hit with a substantial penalty. After all, he should have been enrolled in Medicare 20 years ago. Nope, not so. So long as he can prove he's been covered by a large group plan (and he could), he never needed to enroll in any part of Medicare. Part A came attached to his Social Security when he claimed at age 70, but that was it. He's married to a woman 22 years younger who works for a large company. When he retired, he joined her large employer plan as a spouse. He will not need to sign up for Medicare until she leaves her job. He couldn't believe it, but her employer confirmed his coverage. They will both enroll in Medicare when she retires and loses her group coverage.

- "Antonio" has dual citizenship. Born in Italy to an American mother and Italian father, he relishes a foot in two amazing countries. His wife "Suzie" only has American citizenship and is five years younger. He was concerned how he would cover his younger wife on his Medicare plan. And did he need to be on Medicare at all? In Europe, health care is funded by the government. No need to buy insurance plans. They will spend four or five months a year in Italy; the rest of the time in the US with their grown children and grandchildren. Theirs was a complicated situation. He did need to buy a full complement of Medicare ingredients, even though he would not necessarily use them if he got most of his care in Italy. Suzie, on the other hand, was five years too young for Medicare. She had to research if an ACA Marketplace plan or an individual, private health insurance plan would work for her. We worked to keep pricing as low as possible, but at $2,250 per month for premiums, they weren't thinking U.S. healthcare was a bargain.

- "Kim" is a naturalized citizen, originally from South Korea. His wife is Chinese and is a legal resident with a green card. They were concerned she would not be eligible for Medicare. She's worked odd jobs through the years, but not enough to earn her 40 Social Security credits for her own independent entitlement. What would her options be after she turned 65? Could she get private insurance or buy an ACA Marketplace plan? Good news here. Since Kim was fully eligible for Social Security based on his work record, that also makes his wife eligible for Social

Security benefits as a spouse. And, when you qualify for Social Security, you automatically are eligible for Medicare. Both will be covered on Medicare when each individually reaches 65.

Your situation and options for your complete Medicare will depend on your unique set of circumstances. These are simply examples to illustrate the complexity of individual Medicare situations.

CREATING YOUR MEDICARE RECIPE

SECTION 2:

GROCERY SHOPPING FOR PARTS, PIECES, & FILLING YOUR GROCERY BAG

CREATING YOUR MEDICARE RECIPE

CHAPTER 5

Medicare Part A—The Butter & Sugar

At this point in your Medicare plan, you have laid out the ingredients you'll need to make major decisions on your counter. Think of these key parts and pieces as the base to your complete health care insurance coverage. The same way the butter and sugar, flour, and eggs are the base to your chocolate chip cookies.

Let's face it, without butter and sugar, you can't really make a chocolate chip cookie. Without Medicare Part A, you'd have no major health insurance coverage at all.

Universal health insurance

From the beginning of Medicare, the goal of Part A was to cover every older American citizen with an insurance plan for hospitalization and subsequent skilled nursing care. This was called "universal health insurance" and to qualify, the only requirements[11] were:

- You must personally reach age 65 and be a U.S. resident, and

- You are a U.S. citizen; or, a foreign-born person who has been lawfully admitted to the U.S. for permanent residence and has been residing in the United States for 5 continuous years prior to the month of filing an application for Medicare. Or,

- You are disabled, or
- You have end-stage renal disease (ESRD) or ALS (Amyotrophic lateral sclerosis).

(Note: this book only covers Medicare for those 65+ and retired. These rules are complex enough. For those with disabilities, ALS or ESRD, the rules are different and require a different level of expertise. Seek professional experts who specialize in these areas for your situation.)

That's it. Every U.S. citizen or lawful resident is able to get Medicare Part A. This protects both the individual and their family from financial ruin and ensures every hospital of receiving payment when seniors need hospitalization.

Furthermore, there will be no charge *in the form of a premium* so long as the individual is:

- Eligible for Social Security retirement benefits or Railroad Retirement Benefits (RRB) because they paid at least a minimum of FICA taxes during their working years. (You may know this requirement as meeting your 40 credits in Social Security.) Or,
- Married to a person who is eligible for Social Security or RRBs.

Combining the butter and the sugar

Bakers use the term "creaming" when they combine butter and sugar. It's commonly the first step in making cookie dough. Once you thoroughly cream your butter and sugar together, there's no unmixing these two ingredients.

Think of that with Medicare Part A and Social Security. These two different, yet critical ingredients are creamed together into one mixture. And they cannot be separated.

Why? Because that's how the laws were written. There was already a reliable system in place for employers to pay Social Security FICA when Medicare became part of the law. There was no need to create a wholly new process and system. Instead, Medicare Part A FICA could be incorporated into the existing Social Security operations.

The additional steps to implement Medicare were relatively easy. The federal government established a new HI Trust Fund for Hospitalization Insurance. And employers increased FICA withholdings for the new tax. Social Security and HI were combined together like butter and sugar when Medicare Part A was established.

FICA taxes cover both Social Security and Medicare Part A
Most workers find that paying FICA taxes throughout their working years entitles them to both a Social Security retirement benefit and premium-free Part A. In order to be "fully insured," and therefore eligible for premium-free Part A, you must pay FICA taxes for 40 or more quarters. This covers you and your spouse. A qualifying divorced spouse also gets premium-free Part A as does a widow(er).

You can see how many credits you've earned on your Social Security statement. Set up your own *mySocialSecurity* account at SSA.gov.

Both you and your employer pay FICA taxes. Today, Social Security FICA payments are taxed only up to a certain amount of salary. In 2025, that cap, called the taxable wage base, is $176,100. If you earn more than that amount, you do not continue to pay FICA into Social Security.

However, you do pay Medicare Part A FICA on all your earnings. If you make a million dollars this year, that's great! You'll owe a 1.45% Medicare Part A FICA tax on all $1 million of your wages. Furthermore, you'll also owe a high-income Medicare Part A surcharge. Single-filers earning more than $200,000 and married-couples filing jointly earning more than $250,000, pay an extra 0.9% on wages above those thresholds.

If you or your spouse does not have 40 credits, you can still get Medicare Part A. However, you will pay a hefty monthly premium. The premium changes every year and you'll find that information on Medicare.gov. But to give you an idea, the Part A premium in 2025 was $285 per person per month if you or your spouse had at least 30 credits and $518 per person per month if you or your spouse had less than 30 quarters of coverage.

You'll notice I'm not saying "spouse or partner" here. That is not an oversight. Unless you are legally married (same-sex or opposite-sex marriage), you must individually qualify for your own premium-free Medicare Part A. Your partner cannot cover you on his or her 40 credits. In some uncommon cases, certain couples who live together and hold themselves out as a married couple may be considered "married" for purposes of Medicare or Social Security spousal or survivor benefits. You must contact the Social Security Administration to discuss your personal situation.

Part A is not the same as Part B
You may also notice that I've been quite diligent and specific talking about Medicare Part A in this section. Noting how you need 40 Social Security credits for premium-free Part A. Or, paying FICA for Medicare Part A. Also not a misstep.

The rules for Part A of Medicare are wildly different from Part B. We'll cover Part B in the next chapter. These two parts of Medicare are simply two different ingredients needed to make cookie batter. The combined butter and sugar is not the same as the flour.

Your Medicare Part A FICA taxes are deposited into the HI Trust Fund, managed by the Social Security Administration (SSA). Part A only covers hospitalization insurance (HI), skilled nursing, and hospice. It is completely separate from Part B.

Medicare Part A—The Butter & Sugar

Medicare Part A is premium-free, not free-free
It is so frustrating for so many to learn the reality of Medicare's cost-sharing design. "Part A," they say authoritatively, "is free. I've been paying taxes for decades." Yup, ya sure have been. But I'm the lucky one who gets to tell them they're wrong.

Part A is "PREMIUM-FREE." That is not the same as "FREE-FREE." That extra word in front of free is really meaningful.

You are correct that you've been paying FICA since your first paycheck. However, those FICA taxes only entitle you Part A with no monthly premium. You will, however, encounter any number of "usage fees."

When you are admitted to a hospital—whether for surgery, an illness, a health shock—you will be billed for a deductible. These are the first dollars owed for your hospital stay. In 2025, the Part A deductible is $1,676 per benefit period.

After you pay your share and have a bed—not a private room, but a bed—your Part A will pick up the rest of your hospitalization facility charges for up to 60 days. Hopefully, you'll be in and out in just a few days, but just in case you have a serious condition, you are covered for 60 days. After that you have to pay a share of the cost of the room until day 90. In 2025, that share is $419 per day. And, heaven forbid you are in even longer, you'll pay $838 up to day 150.

Then, you'd pay 100% of the daily costs. This is why people talk about how Medicare does not pay for long-term care. Because it doesn't. Staying in a hospital is not meant to be your living arrangement in old age.

A note about "benefit periods" with Part A. The $1,676 deductible is not how much you would pay for the year of comings and goings into a hospital. A benefit period relates to the reason you have been admitted to the hospital. You can have more than one benefit period per year!

For example, if you are admitted to the hospital for a surgery in January 2025, you'd pay the first $1,676. Then in May 2025, you are in a car accident requiring a separate hospital stay. That's another $1,676 out of your pocket. In November 2025, you have a major health situation landing you in the hospital again. Yes, another $1,676.

Skilled Nursing also comes with usage costs
Many people who have a hospital stay also need some time in a skilled nursing facility. Especially as we get older and more frail. Being moved to a skilled nursing facility where you'll get round the clock care and management of your recovery is typical. After at least a 3-day stay in a hospital, you may go directly to skilled nursing. The first 20 days are paid for by Medicare Part A.

And if you need more than 20 days? You'll pay a share of the daily cost, up to day 100. The Medicare rate in 2025 is $209.50/day. That's $16,760 out of your pocket if you need a 100-day stay.

Once you get close to day 100, there is a lot of talk about getting you home. You typically cannot stay in a skilled nursing facility longer. If a bed continues to be available, and you need more time, you will pay 100% of the daily rate. More often, you will need to move to a nursing home on a full-time basis. Again, this is why Medicare is so upfront about the fact that they do not provide long-term care. They don't.

There is also limited coverage under Part A for some home-health services. After a hospital stay, you may be discharged to go home, but still need some medical care. A home-health aid would come directly to your home to perform the medical care needed. That is often the preferred method of recovery after certain hospital stays for more minor surgeries or situations.

Other Part A coverage: hospice care
Your Medicare Part A becomes very important at the end of your life. Many people need to move into hospice care to stay comfortable in their last days and months. Whether you want to die at home or in another location, hospice care is covered under Medicare Part A. There is a lot to this remarkable service. It covers everything from providing a hospital bed to paying for and administering critical drugs to manage pain. The program also makes sure your medical equipment (such as oxygen and IVs) is set up properly and paid for. Plus, there are resources available to give the caregiver, usually family or friends, a break from time to time.

You discuss hospice care needs with a team of medical professionals. They will guide you through the process, assign medical staff, and help get everything set up within the Medicare Part A rules.

Paying your Part A usage costs
Before you lose sleep over the potential for high usage costs when you or your loved ones need hospitalization, skilled nursing care, or hospice, remember about other Medicare ingredients in your recipe. These Part A costs are just the facts. And you are responsible for paying for them. Either out of your own pocket, or by buying a Medigap plan.

You can also select a Medicare Advantage plan. There are co-pays you will be responsible for, and the costs are structured differently from Original Part A. But there is a maximum out-of-pocket cost in these Part C plans—$9,350 in 2025 for in-network services.

Keep reading for information on how to buy additional insurance to cover your share of the costs.

CREATING YOUR MEDICARE RECIPE

CHAPTER 6

Medicare Part B— Time to Add the Flour

Bread is the staff of life in many cultures and serves as life-saving food. Flour is its key ingredient. And certainly important to making chocolate chip cookie dough.

Part B of Medicare acts like the flour. It is the part of your health insurance that pays the people who can quite literally keep you alive. Every time you see a doctor or a health professional for something that ails you, the lion's share of their charges will be paid for with Part B.

In fact, Part B pays 80% of the Medicare-approved charges from your doctors. Your share is only 20%. Same split for outpatient procedures. If you need a cane or walker, or a scooter, or most other types of durable medical equipment (DME), Part B pays 80% or more of the costs.

Part B is used the most throughout retirement.

How Part B works
Once your Part B is in place, it works just like the insurance card you have today from an employer-sponsored health insurance plan or ACA Marketplace plan. You'll bring it to your doctor and other healthcare appointments. And to the pharmacy or specialty equipment store if you are buying durable medical equipment.

That little red, white, and blue Medicare card with your Part A and Part B number is your ticket to getting the healthcare you need in retirement. The physician's billing group will submit your claim directly to Medicare for payment. You will only get a bill in two situations:

1. This is your first healthcare visit of the year. Before Medicare pays the bill, you are required to pay a portion of the cost first. This is called "first dollars in" and was written into the Medicare law effective in 2020. Your Part B deductible is the first dollars in. In 2025, it was the first $257 of your Part B services. This is an annual charge. Once you pay your share, you won't see another bill, unless...

2. ...you don't have any supplemental Medigap insurance. In that case, you are on the hook for your 20% share of all Part B costs for the year.

Note: If you have a Medicare Advantage plan, you pay the premium for Medicare Part B, but you may or may not need to meet the standard deductible. Each plan determines if there will be a medical deductible and how much it will be. A plan cannot charge more than Medicare's annual deductible. However, it's important to keep in mind that you essentially pay "first dollars in" all year. The services you use generally come with a copay. Or you may be charged a percentage of the cost of the service (co-insurance). You are typically charged more for out-of-network services than in-network services. That is something you'll need to keep a close eye on throughout your retirement if you choose a Medicare Advantage plan. You'll pay these nickel and dime costs until you reach the OOP maximum. $9,350 in 2025 for in-network, $14,000 for in- and out-of-network costs.

Part B is definitely not free-free or premium-free
In the previous chapter, we covered how there is a lot of confu-

sion about Part A's pricing. It is premium-free for most people, but not free-free. Now, with Part B, you'll see how nothing's free. Paying premiums has been in place since Medicare was introduced in 1965. Yet it still angers some people and catches almost everyone off guard.

At the beginning of Medicare, seniors and the federal government split the total premium 50/50. You'd pay half of the premium and Medicare, via the federal government, would pay the other half. But the share from Medicare did not come from the HI Trust Fund. That was strictly for Part A—hospitalization insurance. Instead, seniors paid a monthly premium for their share of Part B costs from their personal money and the rest came from general tax revenues.

In 1966, each person's premium was $3.00. In 2006, monthly premiums reached $88.50 per person per month[12]. In 2025, the Part B standard premium is $185.00.

Table 6. Medicare Part B standard premiums since inception. Per person, per month.

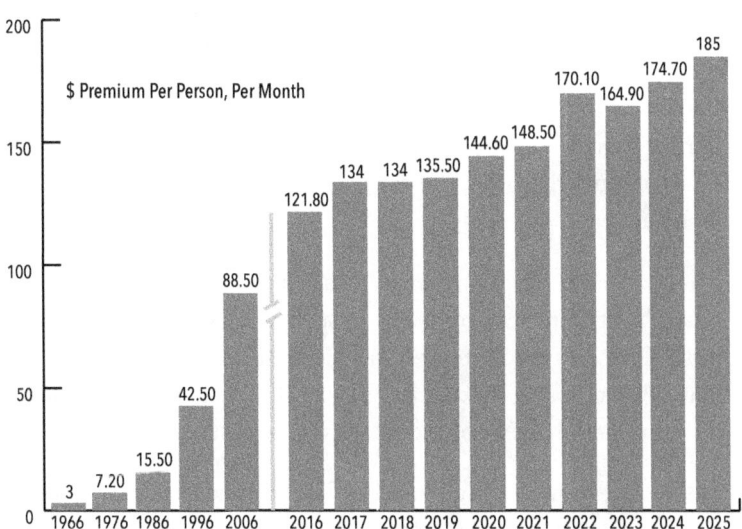

CREATING YOUR MEDICARE RECIPE

You can see the mounting premium payments each person in Medicare Part B is responsible for. But it's also fascinating to see that all retirees have always had to contribute to a premium. Not free-free. Not premium-free.

You are getting a subsidy for your use of the medical system
The financial concept behind insurance is risk-sharing or risk-pooling. Everyone pays something into the pot each month. In the Medicare health insurance world, everyone, whether healthy or sick, younger (65) or older (85+), regardless of which state they live in, or their zip code, or their income and assets, pays the same into the pot. That's the base premium for Part B. For folks with very low income, there are programs to help pay for Medicare premiums.

Many people think it's difficult for retirees on a fixed income to pay for health insurance. What is missing, however, is understanding the full premium amount. Hint…it's not $185.00.

What is happening behind the scenes is some fascinating accounting. Each individual pays only 25% of the total premium for Part B services. The general tax revenue pays the other 75%. Said another way, we're getting a 75% subsidy on Part B services.

Backing into the approximate full cost to cover each Medicare Part B beneficiary, you'll find the total premium is roughly $740 per month, or $8,880 for the year in 2025. Expect it will be higher each following year.

What's needed to make sense of all these premiums is how much healthcare services really cost. It's not such a bitter pill to swallow when you understand the math. You pay $2,220 in Part B premiums instead of roughly $8,800 on average without insurance—only 25% of the total average cost.

Hopefully, you wouldn't need to spend that much on your healthcare services. Everyone should be so lucky as to be healthy and age well. Sadly, millions will need more than their "share." But we are all in this together. That's the purpose of insurance. So when your mom or dad needs a $350,000 procedure next year, or your husband gets a cancer diagnosis and his treatments will be north of $800,000, they'll be on the hook for their $2,220 share of the premium and a $257 Part B deductible.

Not a bad deal at all when you know the facts and stats behind the premiums.

Meet IRMAA

Not everyone will only pay 25% of the average total Part B premium. There's more to the story. Some folks in retirement will meet IRMAA. Meeting IRMAA is going to be an unwelcome and not-so-happy meeting.

"IRMAA" stands for Income-Related Monthly Adjustment Amount. It is an additional premium high-income earners in retirement must pay for their Medicare Part B. If your income as reported on IRS Form 1040 exceeds a particular threshold, you'll get less of a subsidy for your Part B premiums.

The formula is simple and straightforward. In 2025, the threshold is $212,000 in modified adjusted gross income (MAGI) for married couples filing jointly, and $106,000 for individual filers. When your MAGI is higher than the base threshold, there are five IRMAA tiers that indicate how much less of the subsidy you're entitled to:

- IRMAA tier 1 = a 65% subsidy.
- IRMAA tier 2 = a 50% subsidy.
- IRMAA tier 3 = a 35% subsidy.
- IRMAA tier 4 = a 20% subsidy.
- IRMAA tier 5 = a 15% subsidy.

CREATING YOUR MEDICARE RECIPE

You may have heard Part B premiums are means tested. The more means you have in your retirement years, the less subsidy you are eligible for.

Each year, usually by late October, Medicare updates the base premium and the IRMAA table (See Table 7). The income brackets increase with inflation and the premiums increase as well. But the subsidy percentages remain the same unless Congress changes them. You'll find the most current premiums on Medicare.gov.

Table 7. 2025 Part B premiums based on Modified Adjusted Gross Income and tax filing status.

Married Filing Jointly MAGI	Part B Premium Per Person Per Month	Single Filer MAGI
$212,000 or less	$185.00	$106,000 or less
$212k-$266k	$259.00	$106k-$133k
$266k-$334k	$370.00	$133k-$167k
$334k-$400k	$480.90	$167k-$200k
$400k-$750k	$591.90	$200k-$500k
$750k+	$628.90	$500k+

Determining your Part B premium
The Social Security Administration (SSA) runs the numbers each year and sends your Part B premium to you in a "determination letter." It arrives in late November or early December. The SSA looks at your adjusted gross income from two years ago and adds in any non-taxable interest to calculate your Medicare MAGI.

Importantly, we are not talking about your overall net worth here. The determination for your Part B premium is only from income as reported on your IRS Form 1040. It's based on your most recent income available at the IRS, which generally is from two years ago. (If you've filed an extension, your income may be based on three years ago.)

An example: The 2025 Part B premiums were calculated in late 2024. At that time, the SSA pulled your most current tax returns from the IRS, which were from the first quarter of 2024. Those returns reported your 2023 income. Hence, Part B premiums and IRMAA are based on your income two years in arrears.

Take a close look at the lines on the front of the 1040. Your "income" comes from wages or other taxable compensation, pension income, annuity income, interest and dividends, rental income (not passive rental income), and Social Security. For many folks, it's their IRA, 401(k), 403(b), 457 withdrawals and any options paid or nonqualified deferred compensation that makes up the largest part of income. Plus conversions to a Roth IRA and capital gains from the sale of a house or other property count as income. Also added back in for the purposes of determining if you will meet IRMAA this year: any non-taxable interest from municipal bonds or other qualifying investments.

Your Part B premium can change every year
Determining your income for any given year is based on the resources you have coming into your household. You may have wild swings in your income from year to year. Especially in the first few years of retirement. You may be having a lot of fun going places and making up for lost time. To pay for this fun, you may be taking sizeable distributions from your tax-deferred IRAs, driving up your MAGI.

Later in retirement you could also have a sizeable change in income and meet IRMAA. This is an unwelcome surprise for a married person who becomes a widow(er). Your tax filing status changes from married filing jointly to filing single. The income thresholds are much lower for single filers, yet overall income often stays about the same.

Plan for Part B premium changes each year. You might be able to manage some of your income streams to reduce or avoid IRMAA. Or at least you will be prepared for the fluctuations.

Your Social Security payments are automatically reduced for Part B premiums

Paying for Part B is not a welcome expense in anyone's retirement budget. The SSA automatically deducts your Part B standard premium and any IRMAA surcharges from your Social Security payments.

That can also be a surprise if you were expecting say, $2,400 per month from Social Security to pay your bills, but instead you only get $2,200 or $2,000. That's real money you were planning on for living expenses.

The automatic reductions happen once you have both Social Security and Medicare Part B up and running. If you wait to enroll in Social Security until after age 65, but start Medicare Part B at 65, Medicare sends you a quarterly bill. You'll need to pay the bill, in full, before the due date. Late payments can kick you into the penalty zone within a short time period.

If you don't pay Part B premiums on time, your insurance could lapse, and you would be fully responsible for 100% of the services used. Not only your customary 20% Part B share.

Furthermore, if you ever go without continuous health insurance coverage, you could wind up paying penalties when you do get back into Medicare. But you must wait until the first quarter of the year to reenter Part B at all.

What if you don't agree with the determination?
One of the most asked questions I get is "Do I have to pay

the Medicare bill if I disagree with the premium amount?" The answer is a definite YES! Do not mess with Medicare. There are some 58 million people age 65+ enrolled in the program as of 2022, with some 30 million Baby Boomers set to hit 65 soon. Medicare is a gigantic program operating with old computer systems, not enough staff, and way too many complex situations.

Don't skip paying the bill, including IRMAA charges. If you don't agree with the determination, that's fine. There is a well-oiled process for you to dispute your premiums. Many people find they need to do that for several years after retiring.

It is simple and easy to fill out the SSA-44 form and send it to the address listed. Or call your local Social Security office and ask for a redetermination. There are eight reasons your premium will get a second look. Keep in mind you only have 60 days to request a redetermination of your premium once you receive your determination letter.

Remember, your Part B premium will be calculated based on your income two years in arrears. But if you just retired, your income may be lower than it was while working. That is a legitimate reason to ask for a redetermination. If you've reduced your work schedule to part time and your income will be considerably less than two years ago, ask for a second look. The other reasons include: divorce or annulment, marriage, death of your spouse, loss of income producing property, loss of pension income, and employer settlement payment.

What is not generally considered to reduce IRMAA is a Roth conversion from two years ago. Your income was artificially high that year. But the assessment will likely be: if you could afford to do a big Roth conversion and pay the associated tax bill, you can afford to pay higher Part B premiums for a year. Same goes if you got a payout on company stock, options, or nonqualified deferred compensation. Even though it's annoying and you may be mad, remember how the subsidies are meant to work. Higher income folks are not entitled to the maximum 75% subsidy.

You may be in a situation where you're only paying IRMAA for one or two years. Your Part B premium gets recalculated every year based on the income from your most recent tax returns, two years in arrears. It's only when you have high, sustained income that you'll end up in an IRMAA tier throughout retirement.

CHAPTER 7
Medicare Part D—Adding the Eggs

Open up a carton of eggs and pull out two for your chocolate chip cookie recipe. The eggs bind the other ingredients together. Eggs are a critical component of your cookie recipe along with that little tsp of vanilla for added flavor.

Your prescription drugs are like the carton of eggs. Some of you will only have one egg in the carton, others will have a dozen and then some.

Most seniors (89%) take some prescriptions for managing chronic conditions. Best estimates are that 54% of those 65 and older take four prescriptions or more[13].

Does your current health insurance plan offer "creditable" coverage?
In a nutshell, everyone is required to sign up for a Part D plan when they first lose other creditable coverage or pay permanent penalties when joining late. "Creditable" coverage—another technical term—means that the drug plan you have is at least as comprehensive as a Medicare Part D plan and pays as much toward your drugs.

If you are 65+ and get Rx coverage from your employer or your spouse's or partner's employer, you need to find out if the plan is creditable. Usually, large employers offer creditable coverage as do many mid-sized companies. But many small companies do not offer such extensive coverage for their employees, and therefore, your plan may not be creditable under Medicare. Some high-deductible health plans do not qualify as offering creditable coverage.

Employers are required to send an annual notice reporting if the plan is considered creditable for Medicare. If it is, you can keep that plan, even if you are 65 or older and as long as you are enrolled in the group plan. However, as soon as you lose creditable coverage, you only have 63 days to get your Part D up and running.

Very important: You cannot get a Part D plan without having Part A and/or Part B in place. Part D is an "add-on" to your Medicare recipe. Social Security takes up to 60 days to set up your Medicare Part A and Part B plan and send you your card. Plan ahead!

Part D plans are generally inexpensive, but IRMAA applies here too

The good news for most folks is Part D plan premiums are quite inexpensive relative to Part B premiums. For those who need only a few generic or low-cost prescriptions, the monthly premiums might only be $10 or $25. You'll buy a Part D plan from a private insurer available in your zip code. Paying the monthly premium gives you access to prescription drug coverage and negotiated rates for the Rx's you do take. You will pay this monthly premium directly to the insurance company you've selected.

The not-so-good news is that if you have higher income in retirement, you're going to meet IRMAA again. As with Medicare Part B, Part D is also subsidized by the federal government. But, when your income is high, you are not entitled to the highest subsidies. You will need to pay an additional IRMAA premium to Medicare. The monthly amount assessed will also be automatically pulled from your Social Security payment each month or you will get a bill in the mail.

This means, if you have high income in retirement, you are paying two separate Part D premiums. One directly to the insurance company of your choice. The other to Medicare.

According to CMS, about 92% of those with a Part D plan pay $0 to Medicare. They may pay a monthly premium to their Part D private insurer.

The other 8% will meet Part D IRMAA. This charts gives you an example of Part D IRMAA charges. Both brackets and amounts change every year. You'll find the current year's information on Medicare.gov generally by late September or October.

Table 8. Part D IRMAA table for 2025.

Married Filing Jointly MAGI	Part D Additional Premium Per Person Per Month	Single Filer MAGI
$212,000 or less	$0	$106,000 or less
$212k-$266k	$13.70	$106k-$133k
$266k-$334k	$35.30	$133k-$167k
$334k-$400k	$57.00	$167k-$200k
$400k-$750k	$78.60	$200k-$500k
$750k+	$85.80	$500k+

Shop for the cheapest Part D plan

The way this Medicare ingredient works is commercial insurance companies offer plans to help you pay for your medications. Otherwise, you'd be fully responsible for paying for your prescriptions. If you want a Part D insurance plan to help share the costs, you'll pay a monthly premium to join a plan.

While it might be reasonable to think you get what you pay for when it comes to prescription drugs, turns out, it is not. You want to find the one Part D plan that includes the exact drugs you take at the lowest cost. You're looking for the combination of lowest monthly premium plus cost of your specific drugs. It is that simple. Or is it?

Not all Part D plans cover all your drugs
It is usually easy to find the lowest cost Part D plan using Medicare's "find plans" tool on Medicare.gov. Behind the scenes, there is a massive database of drug cost information from each insurance company. Each insurer decides how much to charge for the drugs carried on their list, called the formulary. They also decide if they are going to cover the all the drugs in a specific category. And, they don't have to.

Insurers are required to play by the CMS rules, but because there are thousands of different drugs with different dosages, there is some flexibility. The insurer must carry at least two drugs in each of a number of categories, but they don't need to offer all drugs in any given category.

For treating depression, for example, there might be 15 different drug options available in the market. Your doctor prescribed two specific drugs. When you shop for those two specific drugs, they may not be covered on all the insurer's plans. Maybe WellCare covers both drugs, but you've been using SilverScripts for years and now they do not cover one of the drugs. No worry. You'll simply switch to WellCare to get coverage for both necessary drugs. Or you stay with SilverScripts and pay full retail price for that second drug.

Note the pharmacies
Let me offer a big caution when it comes to shopping for your Part D drug plan. Buried deep in the opaqueness of this entire process is a third party: the pharmacies. Unknown to most of us, the pharmacies are a gigantic player in Part D plans. The

Medicare Part D—Adding the Eggs

manufacturers, insurers, and pharmacies all coordinate on pricing. There is no obvious rhyme or reason...except to say each is a business and each is focused on maximizing profitability.

For you, the unsuspecting American consumer, you simply must get in the game here and make sure you are getting the best price for your egg carton filled with drugs. And that means looking at all the pharmacies in your area. Different pharmacy chains have negotiated different costs for the same drugs.

No one is going to tell you. And, frankly, from a business perspective, the more you overpay for your drugs, the better. For the big players. Not for you.

Here's specifically what I'm talking about. Most people are loyal to their local pharmacies. You're either a CVS fan or a Walgreens fan, you prefer Walmart or you like Target better. You like to pick up your Rx's in person in case you have questions. And you can buy other stuff you need during this quick trip to the pharmacy. I'm going to strongly suggest it's time to rethink that very way of running your weekly errands.

Behind the scenes, each pharmacy chain is making deals with the insurers and manufactures about pricing. Or the chain is owned by an insurance company. Those who cut the best deals are "in-network, preferred" pharmacies. Mail order is often in this best-price category. Those whose deals aren't quite as good may still be "in-network," but not preferred. And those on what I call the "naughty list" can still sell the drugs you need, but they are "out-of-network," and you'll pay a whooping lot more.

Two examples with eye-popping results
I track costs for a number of different drugs each year in several zip codes. The example shown here is for zip code 02360, Plymouth County, Massachusetts. You are looking at a range of costs for the exact same two drugs—two generic blood pres-

sure Rx's. There is a low-cost Part D plan, a medium-cost plan, and a high-cost plan. These were the available prices at different pharmacies.

Table 9. Costs of two generic drugs in 2025, zip code 02360

	Monthly Premium	Annual Premium	Annual Deductible	Total Annual Cost: Premium + Cost of 2 generic drugs in 2025				
				Walgreens	CVS	Big Y	Walmart	Mail Order
Lowest-cost plan: WellCare Value Script	$12.40	$149	$590	Preferred $149	Preferred $149	Out-of-Network $717	In-Network $305	Preferred $149
Medium-cost plan: Silver Script Choice	$50.70	$608	$590	In-Network $656	In-Network $661	In-Network $659	In-Network $736	In-Network $649
Higher-cost plan: Blue Medicare Rx Premier	$190.80	$2,290	$0	In-Network $2,426	Preferred $2,314	In-Network $2,360	Preferred $2,314	In-Network $2,298

What you see is nothing short of astonishing. And highly disturbing. For the exact same two drugs, you could pay $149 at CVS for the entire year or over $2,400 at Walgreens. And you would never know if you didn't do your homework.

And this isn't even the most interesting part of the Part D drug cost story…

In this example from San Jose County, California, zip code 95125, I looked at the same two generic drugs from the prior example and added in a "designer" drug, the heavily advertised Dupixent. I was curious about brand-name drugs that have huge advertising budgets behind them. Clearly folks need these expensive drugs, but how expensive are they?

Medicare Part D—Adding the Eggs

Table 10. Costs of two generic drugs + Dupixent in 2025, zip code 95125

	Monthly Premium	Annual Premium	Annual Deductible	Total Annual Cost: Premium + Cost of 2 generic drugs + Dupixent in 2025				
				Bascon Pharmacy	CVS	Enborg Lane Pharmacy	Walgreens	Mail Order
Lowest-cost plan: Cigna Healthcare Assurance Rx	$1.80	$21.60	$590	Out-of-Network $55,356	In-Network $2,022	Out-of-Network $55,356	Preferred $2,022	Preferred $2,022
Medium-cost plan: AARP Medicare Rx Preferred from UHC	$115.40	$1,385	$0	In-Network $3,263	In-Network $3,313	Out-of-Network $56,719	Preferred $3,303	Preferred $3,288
Higher-cost plan: Blue Shield Rx Enhanced	$183.50	$2,202	$0	Out-of-Network $57,536	Preferred $4,059	In-Network $4,061	In-Network $4,064	In-Network $4,059

In short, you need to be extremely careful about the combined pharmacy and drug plan you choose. In this particular case, you might pay about $2,000 for the year's supply of all three drugs...or over $57,000! It's your choice. And it's up to each individual person to reassess their Rx's, their plans, *AND* the pharmacy every year they're in Medicare.

Thanks to the Inflation Reduction Act of 2022, retirees will be capped at $2,000 per year for their out-of-pocket covered drugs. Going forward, they'll need to keep a close eye on the premium cost as well. Furthermore, if someone uses an out-of-network pharmacy, the $2,000 cap for covered drugs will not apply. They will pay retail prices.

Can your 95 year-old parent really deal with this mess?
Honestly, I don't much care that there are back room deals going on and renegotiations every year. That is part of business.

We all want higher earnings on these drug stocks and pharmacy chains when we invest in them. That's not the key issue.

The issue here is that we expect the oldest Americans to figure out who cut which deal this year and who landed on the naughty list. This is some of the most abhorrent behavior we have going on in healthcare. For your granny, gramps, mom, or dad to be forced to figure out a clandestine process so he or she can afford their drugs is nothing short of sinful. And frankly, reprehensible. And all the cooks in this kitchen know this is going on.

The ones who don't know are our 80-year olds. And 90-year-olds. And all those we celebrate when they reach their 100th birthday. While those with a Part D plan or a Medicare Advantage plan receive an Annual Notice of Change (ANOC), these are not readable documents. They contain legally required information, but most folks are simply not going to read them or understand them.

It is known and well-documented that the vast majority of older Americans do not reshop their Part D plans. Ever. So when their pharmacy moves from preferred to in-network or out-of-network, they have no idea. Their generic medicine that cost $2 per month last year, now costs $27. Or a $30 tier two drug is now $812. Per month. They had no idea at all. And they are stuck for the next 12 months before they can find a new Part D plan.

While lots of older Americans use computers regularly, it's not easy to figure out how to work Medicare's plan finder tool and understand how critical it is to look at every pharmacy chain offered in a radius of five to ten miles surrounding your home.

Referencing the two examples shown, there is quite a collection of pharmacies one can choose. In zip code 02360 there are 8 pharmacies within 5 miles and 18 within 10 miles. But in zip code 95125, there are only 2 pharmacies within one mile. But those residents can choose from 107 pharmacies within 5 miles. Well, that's nuts.

These shenanigans are simply too complex, complicated, and downright conniving to foist upon our oldest, and often sickest, Americans.

Furthermore, lots of insurers have been buying up pharmacies. So there is no real competition. The three or four gigantic players are mucking around with pricing. Adding insult to injury are the Pharmacy Benefit Managers—middlemen who cut deals between the various players adding layers of costs to your drugs. Watch what is going on over the next 10 years with the structure of the drug industry. And the cost of your own prescriptions. It should be fascinating.

Arm yourself for your future years
It's important to understand how involved you'll need to be in your medical and prescription insurance as you age. Especially with the Part D plans whether you have a standalone plan or drug coverage built into a Medicare Advantage plan. You will reshop your plans every single year. Between October 15th and December 7th, you can change your drug plan every year. And it's likely you will change plans frequently. Even when you haven't added or dropped a drug. The dosage hasn't changed. You don't take more or less than you did last year.

To put it bluntly, it's not about you. It's all about the craziness that goes on behind the scenes. There's a big party next door, but you aren't invited. You're just left to clean up the mess.

So, mark your calendar for every November 1st to reshop your plans. This is the only way you can ensure you aren't paying too much at pharmacy X when the exact same drug would cost 95% less at pharmacy Y.

Do you even need to bother with a Part D plan?
Excellent question. I'm surprised more people don't ask that question. The people who ask are always the ones who don't need any prescription drugs. And, for them, sadly, the answer is yes. The answer is also yes for everyone else on Medicare.

Embedded in Medicare Part B and Part D are permanent penalties for enrolling late. With Part D you would be considered late to the party if you join more than 63 days after other creditable coverage has ended.

To avoid any penalties, and any gaps in coverage, you generally must join a Part D drug plan within 63 days of joining Medicare. Usually, Medicare starts the first day of the month containing your 65th birthday. But for those who continue to work after age 65 for a large employer, they typically continue to get health insurance plus drug coverage on that group plan. They will have 63 days after leaving a creditable plan to get into a Part D plan.

In general, the rules of the road are that everyone needs a Part D plan, even though it is technically voluntary.

But I have a Medicare Advantage Plan. Do I need a separate Part D plan?
Well, in that case, the answer is no. You cannot have a stand-alone Part D plan with a Medicare Advantage Plan. However, your Medicare Advantage plan comes with a built-in drug plan (MAPD). You'll need to do some serious shopping to find the right combination of a Medicare Advantage plan that covers all your drugs for the lowest total cost while also covering your doctors and hospitals and other healthcare providers you prefer to use.

Even if you do not take any prescription drugs when you sign up initially for Medicare Advantage, you need to buy a plan that does have drug coverage. Do not make the mistake of buying a Part C plan without drug coverage. Penalties will apply years later when you need to switch into a Part C that includes drug coverage.

You'll need to reshop your MAPD every year to make sure all the coordinating parts work again for the following year and cover your prescriptions at the best cost. This is your task each November 1st.

Can I use drug discount cards with my Part D plan?
A relatively new option has surfaced to help everyone pay for their drugs. You may have seen commercials for Singlecare or GoodRx. Or received a discount pharmacy card from AARP. Those and others are specialty coupon programs. You can use these discounts today whether you have employer insurance, an ACA Marketplace plan, or Medicare Part D.

You might want to try out these programs next time you need to order or refill a prescription. Before going to your favorite pharmacy, check for discounts first. It might be that your pharmacy has the lowest price for your particular drug. Or it may be the most expensive. Experiment with your own prescriptions. These discount programs have gained in popularity and may save you a pretty penny.

Once you have a Medicare Part D plan or a Medicare Part C plan, you can indeed use these coupons. However, you cannot combine the two. You can't use your Part D with a GoodRx coupon at the same time. So, you'll have a choice to make. Is it better, faster, cheaper to put your routine prescriptions on the Part D plan? Or would you rather shop around for the best price each month or quarter?

For ease and convenience, if your prescription costs on your Part D plan are in the ballpark of any discount pricing, you're probably better off using your Part D for your recurring Rx's. Otherwise, each time you need a refill, you'll need to contact the prescriber and ask them to change the location of the pharmacy. To save perhaps hundreds of dollars a year, it may be worth your time to shop around for better discounts.

For one-off prescriptions for an illness, you'll want to check for discounts. Try using a discount program for the best prices. They are free to use, and you can download the apps to your smartphone.

Part D notes
To say getting your prescriptions once on Medicare is going to take time, energy, patience, and some expertise is a tremendous understatement. It's more like opening a carton of eggs where some have been hardboiled, some soft-boiled, and others fresh from the hen. Which is which? How will you know? It's going to take time and patience, some experimentation, and a mop to clean up the mess.

When you enter Medicare, do not get locked into using your favorite pharmacy. To get the best prices, it's knowing where the deals are. There are lots of ways to save money on your drugs. Even if you think $15 a month is a reasonable price for your generic drug, you may be paying $14 too much.

Also understand that the prices of your Rx's can change throughout the year. You'll get a short notice from the Part D insurer and then you're on the hook for higher prices for the remaining months in the year.

None of this is okay in my opinion. Right now, no one seems to be actively working on shutting down the back office poker games. It's on each of us to get smarter and work the system the best we can. That it is a ridiculously unfair situation to put our oldest Americans in doesn't seem to be on anyone's radar.

CHAPTER 8

Optional Ingredient that Isn't Really Optional—Medigap

Everyone has a preference about their favorite chocolate chip cookies. Some like lots of chocolate chips, some just a few. Others know that walnuts make the cookies even better versus those who can't stand the thought of adding nuts of any kind. My secret ingredient to the best chocolate chip cookies is raisins. The extra sweetness and texture is awesome. Plus, my family doesn't really like added raisins. Oh well. More for me!

In the case of cookies, there are some optional ingredients. In the case of Medicare, there are optional plans to choose from. However, making sure you have full healthcare coverage once you are on Medicare really isn't optional. Supplemental or optional ingredients are technically voluntary. Except they really aren't.

The Original Medicare supplemental plans: Medigap
As you now know, even when Original Medicare Parts A and B are in place, you pay certain cost-sharing amounts. Private insurance companies designed plans specifically to cover your share. These Medigap plans quite literally pay those costs you would otherwise pay out-of-pocket. You can buy a Medigap plan from a private insurance company such as United Health Care, Humana, Blue Cross, etc. You'll pay a monthly premium to the insurance company, and they pick up your share of Part A and Part B costs.

Every doctor, specialist, outpatient facility, hospital system, etc. that accepts Medicare Parts A and B must also take the Medigap policy you've chosen. These plans offer you the maximum flexibility to go anywhere and see any doctor in the U.S. and U.S. Territories. And you can budget a set amount (the premium) every month. That way, you'll know exactly how much you are spending on healthcare. Plus you can estimate how much the premiums will increase each year with inflation.

Once you have a Medigap plan in place, you can never be kicked out of the plan unless you fail to pay your monthly premium. You never get a bill for the Medicare-covered services you chose to cover in your Medigap plan. And you can be confident that your covered healthcare expenses will be met. Wherever you decide to get services.

How Medigap plans work
Medigap plans are structured in a highly prescriptive manner. The insurance companies offering such plans must conform to exact specifications as determined by CMS—the Centers for Medicare and Medicaid Services. This is the arm of the federal government that oversees all parts of Medicare and makes the rules insurance companies must adhere to.

In the case of Medigap plans, there are eight categories of coverage. There is a minimum category (Medigap Plan A) and a fully-comprehensive category (Medigap Plan G) and a whole bunch more. You decide which categories you want your Medigap insurance plan to pay for. The more coverage you want, the higher your monthly premium. No surprise there.

A particularly confusing area of Medigap plans is how they are titled. In all but three states (Massachusetts, Minnesota, and Wisconsin), the gap plans are called plan A, B, D, G, K, L, M, and N. It is easy to mix up Medicare *Part A* or Medicare *Part B* with Medigap *Plan A* or Medigap *Plan B*. They are not the same. Annoying, but that's what we have to deal with.

Some people with Medigap plans have other lettered plans such as C, F, and I. Those plans were offered in the past but have been retired. You will still see information about plans C and F when researching your choices. Those were the most recent two to be shelved. Why? Congress didn't like the idea that a Medigap plan paid the first dollars on a bill for Medicare Part B services. They changed the law so that each of us must pay a Part B deductible first. It's not a lot of up-front money—$257/year in 2025. But Congress feels better that all the older folks have more skin in the game to pay for their healthcare. And that meant Medigap plans C and F had to be retired, as they covered the Medicare Part B deductible.

However, if an individual is entering Medicare for the first time after age 65, but was 65 before 12/31/2019, he or she is technically still eligible for Medigap plan C or F. Don't fall for that, though! Just because you are grandfathered into these older plan options does not mean they are a good deal. They are priced much higher than the nearly identical plans D and G, except for the $257 Part B deductible.

Generally, you'll pay about $500 - $600 per year more for the retired Plans C or F versus paying your own Part B deductible of $257. Said another way: you're going to pay $600 to an insurance company for a $257 benefit. That is an amazing profit margin for the insurer!

Medigap plans: categories of covered benefits
Each of the lettered gap plans cover a specific number of benefits. Furthermore, every Medigap with the same letter offered by every insurance company must cover the exact benefits in exactly the same way. That way, you can easily and fairly comparison shop. The only differences when you look at Medigap Plan G from insurance company number 1 vs. the Medigap Plan G from insurance company number 2 will be the premium, level of customer service, and 800 number. There cannot be any other differences. By law.

These are the eight cost categories Medigap plans cover:

1. All Medigaps must provide coverage for some Medicare Part A costs. The insurer must cover those costs for an additional year beyond what Medicare Part A covers. The costs covered are co-insurance and daily room charges.

2. Some Medigaps will also cover your hospital deductible. That's $1,676 per event in 2025. If you do not want to get a bill for your share of a hospital stay, you want a Medigap plan that offers Medicare Part A deductible coverage.

3. All Medigaps cover your cost share of the Medicare Part A hospice care benefit. However, not all cover these costs at 100%. One Medigap pays 50%, another Medigap pays 75%. You have to decide if you are willing to pay for some expenses should you need hospice services as you are nearing end of life.

4. Medigaps must cover your Medicare Part B coinsurance costs or copays. That's usually your 20% share of costs for physicians and outpatient services, etc. Two of the gap plans pay less than 100% of your share. You have to decide if you want all of your covered Medicare Part B costs handled by the insurer or if you are comfortable paying for some portion.

5. Only one Medigap pays for physician's "excess charges." That's Medigap Plan G. A physician who accepts Medicare's pricing is stuck with whatever rate Medicare decides to pay. But some physicians' groups charge up to 15% more. No doctor is required to see patients on Medicare. Fortunately, almost all do. Some just charge more than the Medicare assigned rate. You are responsible for the additional charges unless you choose Medigap Plan G.

Optional Ingredient that Isn't Really Optional—Medigap

6. Most Medigaps offer coverage for your share of costs if you are admitted to a skilled nursing facility. Two of the plans will pay 50% or 75% of those costs.
7. In some long-ago compromise made in Congress when they were drafting the Medicare law, all Medigaps must cover the first three pints of blood if you need a transfusion during a surgery. Go figure.
8. None of the Medigaps fully cover foreign travel medical expenses and four plans don't cover any. The other four pay 80% of the costs you may incur. However, this is not coverage you likely need. If you have a health emergency while traveling, most expenses will be paid under Medicare Parts A and B anyway. And, if you are going on a more exotic trip, you can buy travel insurance that is more robust than Medicare, and quite inexpensive. This particular benefit might have been important decades ago, but today there are better options for your travels.

The best way to decide which Medigap plan is right for you is to do your research. First, look at the table provided on Medicare's website— https://www.medicare.gov/health-drug-plans/medigap/basics/compare-plan-benefits . You'll see all gap plans and how they cover your share of costs.

Then, use the Medicare "find plans" tool to see which insurance companies offer Medigap plans in your zip code and county. Link to the tool from Medicare.gov's home page— https://www.medicare.gov/plan-compare/#/?year=2024&lang=en

If you decide a plan N is the best option for you, look at the pricing for the insurers in your area. Is there any reason you should pay more for one insurance company's Medigap plan N than a less expensive plan? Remember all coverage for that lettered plan must be the same.

When to enroll in a Medigap plan

Medigap plans are never retroactive. So it is imperative you have your Medigap plan in place on the same date your Medicare Part B is going into effect. If you are starting Medicare on February 1st, you must have your Medigap in place on February 1st as well to have complete health insurance coverage.

The insurers that sell Medigap plans generally start a Medigap plan on the first day of the month immediately following your application. So, if you need a February 1st start date, you apply for your Medigap in January. It's best if you apply early in the month to allow the insurer time to go through their process. But even if you call to apply on January 31st, your Medigap should start on February 1st.

Coordinating all your ingredients so they get into mixing bowl at exactly the same time is the key to a successful transition into Medicare. That means, you need your Medicare number, your Medicare Part B effective date, and your timely application to get your Medigap plan in place. (You would also do the same with Part D—apply the month immediately prior to your Part B effective date.)

Your one and only one Medigap open enrollment, no questions asked opportunity

Because Medigap plans are so flexible and offer you so much protection, you need to give a little on your end. The insurers must allow you into any Medigap plan you choose, but only at the start of your initial Medicare enrollment. You have one, single, 6-month period to join a Medigap plan with no questions asked, no assessment of your pre-existing conditions, and no health underwriting to see if you have a chronic issue.

The clock starts on your Part B effective date and ends six months later. Period.

If you do not have your Medigap in place on the same day your Part B starts, you likely have no supplemental coverage. At all.

Optional Ingredient that Isn't Really Optional—Medigap

Medigap policies do not cover expenses you incur before the policy is in place. So, if your Medicare Part B starts on April 1st, you technically have a 6-month open window to buy your Medigap plan—until the end of September. However, you will pay any Part A deductible in that time period if you end up in the hospital. And you will pay your 20% share of costs for all Part B services you use.

DO NOT expose yourself to that risk!

The 6-month open period is nice to know about, but do not wait to buy a Medigap plan if you know you are going the Medigap route. Medigap plans do not pay your costs retroactively. Those costs are on you.

In some cases, you may have a secondary insurance policy in place that would temporarily pay some of your costs before your Medigap plan is in place. It might be from an employer or union plan or something similar. But you have to use great caution with these plans and make sure you will be fully covered if you need to use the healthcare system.

Others will have access to other types of insurance that works with Medicare. This includes retired military members and their spouses who have TRICARE for Life. Veterans may have additional coverage through the VA. If you have a state pension it may include some health insurance benefits. Some union retirement health plans do the same. Federal government employees have different options for health insurance in retirement. And there is a Tribal healthcare program for American Indians and Alaska Natives.

In every case, it's up to each individual to review the choices available to them. You'll need to do your research and ask a lot of questions.

Guaranteed Issue – buying a Medigap plan later
There are a few situations that allow individuals to buy a Medi-

gap plan outside of their initial 6-month initial enrollment period without undergoing any medical underwriting. These opportunities are typically if you involuntarily lose your health insurance coverage or have other approved special situations.

Insurance companies do not have to sell you a Medigap plan after your 6-month window. You may be required to go through medical underwriting, where the insurance company will review the details of your medical history. Or, you may have to wait up to six months for a pre-existing condition to be covered under the Medigap plan.

The rules around who qualifies for a guaranteed issue versus who does not vary by state. The best course of action if you missed your initial 6-month open enrollment Medigap window is to contact your State Health Insurance Assistance Program (SHIP representatives). This is a no-cost resource anyone can use to understand the options available for their particular situation. Look for your SHIP group on their website— https://www.shiphelp.org/.

CHAPTER 9

A Substitute to Your Medicare Recipe—Medicare Part C Plans

What if you aren't much of a baker? And baking chocolate chip cookies in your kitchen is not something you do? That's ok. There are other options. You can stop at a bakery. Order online. Or just buy a package next time you're at the grocery store.

Buying a Medicare Part C plan is like buying cookies at the grocery store. It's a completely baked and packaged health insurance plan. All the same basic ingredients are in the already baked cookie, and there might even be a few extras you wouldn't put in your homemade version.

You are substituting individual ingredients for a packaged alternative.

Medicare Advantage is not the same as Medicare or Medigap
Medicare Part C plans are not supplemental plans. They do not sit underneath Medicare Parts A and B to pick up your share of the costs. Instead these plans are a complete replacement to Medicare. They are an all-in-one alternative to you pulling individual ingredients off the shelf.

But from a consumer perspective, Part C plans pretty much look like a supplemental plan when initially buying them. That's because you can't buy one until you have enrolled in Medicare Part A and Part B and are paying your Part B monthly premium plus any IRMAA upcharges. You cannot buy a Medicare Advantage plan (MA) unless and until you are fully enrolled in Medicare Parts A and B.

You also cannot buy a Medicare Advantage Plan and a Medigap plan. It is illegal for someone to sell you a Medigap if you have a Medicare Advantage Plan.

The insurance company has a seat at the table
With Part C plans, the underlying pricing model is different. And, importantly, who controls your care is different. In most cases, your care will be co-shared between the medical experts and the insurance company. This is a significant difference from buying and using a Medigap plan.

You must be comfortable with the fact that your doctor's recommendations will be reviewed and approved or disapproved by the insurance company before you receive care. Before payments are made for specialty care, surgeries, expensive or experimental drug regimens, and any other costly recommendation from your doctor, the insurance company will need to approve the doctor's recommendation. You need to be well armed and prepared to fight for your treatments if you end up with a costly health condition and the care recommendation is denied.

Keep in mind Part C plans are billed and promoted as something unique and a real alternative to "Original Medicare" (Part A + Part B). But in reality, they are wildly complicated insurance products with thousands of rules and stipulations. You'll only find out about these rules if you decide to read the 200+ page documents that support each plan, or get sick and find out your care recommendation has been denied.

Medicare Advantage plans are complex bundled product offerings from an insurance company. They bundle together not only Medicare Parts A and B coverage along with prescription drugs, but also doctors, hospital systems, and specialized healthcare services into a network. And the insurance company has not only a seat at the table, but the chair at the head of the table. The healthcare professionals and systems must agree to be part of the network. That's how they'll get paid.

Who's paying your doctors?
A big difference between "Original" Medicare Parts A and B with a Medigap and a Part D plan and a Medicare Advantage plan arrangement is how the healthcare infrastructure gets paid.

- When you choose Original Medicare + Medigap + Part D, any doctors you see and any hospitals you use are paid first by the federal government (primary payer) under Parts A and B, and the remaining costs by your Medigap plan (secondary payer). Your drugs costs are shared between you and the Part D insurer, the manufacturer, and the federal government.

- When you choose a Medicare Advantage plan with drug coverage (shorthand: MAPD), the healthcare professionals and hospitals are paid by the insurer where they are networked. There is a contractual agreement between the parties. Where does the insurer get the money to pay your doctor? From the federal government by way of Medicare. Drug costs are shared between you and the MAPD.

You don't get involved in pricing. It occurs behind the scenes. However, if you want to go out-of-network after you've bought into a MAPD, you'll be paying out-of-pocket for a larger share of the costs. Or the entire price tag.

The big the insurers were trying to achieve cost control. There's no argument that healthcare costs have been rising too fast for decades. Networking doctors and hospitals to reduce payment rates should reduce costs. In theory.

MAPDs gain traction
It took some years to gain traction, but Medicare Advantage

plans now make up more than 50% of the overall Medicare market. The draw of a $0 monthly premium is too good to resist for half the retirees. The idea of combining health insurance with cost reductions for dental, vision, and hearing is also appealing. Though there is little actual cost benefit to these extra goodies.

Insurance companies have been sweetening the deal in some communities over the years. They might provide cost reimbursement for travel back and forth to medical appointments. Or give members some cash to spend at the local pharmacy. Some plans even offer to pay all or part of one's Medicare Part B premium. But there are lots of requirements and restrictions to meet first. All buried in the fine print. Typically, these additional goods are limited to specific regions or center on lower income retirees.

When first introduced, MAPD plans were called Medicare+Choice. They launched to American consumers 1999. These plans are governed under the Medicare law as Part C.[14]

It was the ability to add in options specifically disallowed in the Medicare law that allowed a name change in 2003. Under the Medicare Modernization Act of 2003, Medicare+Choice became Medicare Advantage.

A snappy marketing name, for sure. But you really have to ask yourself, what advantages am I really getting?

A look under the hood of Medicare Advantage Plans

There's no question our healthcare system is a huge pile of broken cookies. It is crazy complicated and frankly, an absolute mess at this time. So any solution that has the potential to remove complexity is appealing. MAPDs should be just that kind of product.

But they are a far cry from helping older Americans navigate the complex infrastructures of health care. It's critically important that you research these plans and try your best to figure out how they are going to work for you. The plan documents usually include a summary—about 30 pages long. The full documents are 100 – 200 pages. These documents are where you need to spend time to comparison shop before you buy.

No two plans can be fairly compared. Not within a single insurance company. Not across insurers. Whereas Medigap plans must be identical so you can compare apples to apples, MAPDs are as varied as the entire cookie aisle at the biggest grocery stores. You're not just looking for a particular type or brand of cookie. Instead, with MAPDs, it's up to you to compare every ingredient on every box of cookies to decide which will work for you and your health situation.

In most areas of the country, you will have between 35 and 65 different MAPDs to choose from. I'm not kidding. There has been an explosion of these plans, effectively making it impossible for consumers to do any sort of meaningful comparison.

To be fair, it's not that the insurers don't provide comprehensive information. You can relatively easily find the full documents explaining how payments work for every type of care and procedure. So technically, they've met the obligation to provide you with information. But to think any normal, wonderful person will spend the hours required to read, digest, and compare one plan document against another is pretty much unrealistic (or insane).

MAPD HMO or PPO or PFFS?
Further adding to the complexity of choosing your ingredients, MAPDs aren't just one type. They come in several different flavors, all differing by the size and scope of the network they cover. It's like deciding to use hazelnuts or pecans or walnuts or macadamia nuts in your chocolate chip cookies. You're still baking cookies, but the end result won't taste the same.

In the case of MAPDs, most people have a range of structures to choose from including the following:

- **HMO**—Health Maintenance Organization. Individuals must use the network for all healthcare services to get any insurance coverage. If using out-of-network doctors or hospitals, the individual usually pays 100% of costs incurred (except for emergencies).

- **HMO/POS**—Health Maintenance Organization with Point-of-Service option. Individuals are required to use the network, but in certain cases, for certain services, will be able to use an out-of-network provider and still have insurance coverage.

- **PPO**—Preferred Provider Organization. With this type of MAPD, the individual has more flexibility. They have full access to the insurer's network but may also go out-of-network. Using a non-network doctor or service is likely to cost more, but insurance coverage remains available.

- **PFFS—Private Fee-for-Service.** Individuals can go to any Medicare-approved doctor, healthcare provider, or hospital that accepts the plan's payment terms and agrees to treat them. If the plan has a network, any of the network providers are available to them. When using an out-of-network provider, they must accept the plan's terms, and the individual may pay more.

How will you know which option will work best for you? Frankly, it takes a fair amount of time and effort to research each insurer that offers plans in your zip code. You'll want to set up and run cost models so you can estimate how much you'll pay out-of-pocket for a specific type of MAPD.

Two MAPD examples

To give you an idea of how much you could be charged for various types of hospital stays, I ran two examples. One was for a general surgery such as a knee or hip replacement that does not require a hospital stay. And one for a cardiac surgery. There are different cost categories for cardiac issues. I could not get these costs confirmed as the insurance companies offering MAPDs cannot give estimates. You only find out the cost of care once you have a surgery planned and the diagnosis codes are available.

If you are a budgeter, MAPDs are likely to make you a little bit crazy. You might have a $0 monthly premium, but if you get sick and need hospitalization and care, you have no way to know how much it will cost. Except that your out-of-pocket charges will not exceed a stated annual maximum. In 2025, that's $9,350 for in-network costs and $14,000 for in- and out-of-network expenses.

In example 1, I made up a reasonable scenario of steps for someone needing an outpatient surgery. You'll see an estimate for the number of visits and the costs from a 2025 Blue Cross PPO plan document in zip code 02360. Of course, actual numbers will vary so you'll need to do your own research in your zip code. But the bottom line is: MAPDs aren't free. This surgery might cost nearly $1,700.

Table 11: Example 1—Estimated costs in a MAPD for an outpatient surgery, in-network, 2025

	Cost Per Visit	# Visits	Est Cost
Pre-surgical Visits w Specialists	$45	4	$180
X-rays	$10	2	$20
MRI/CT Scan	$365	1	$365
Outpatient Surgery	$275	1	$275
Follow Up Specialist Visits	$45	3	$135
Physical Therapy--1st 6 weeks	$20	18	$360
Physical Therapy--2nd 6 weeks	$20	12	$240
Physical Therapy--3rd 6 weeks	$20	6	$120
TOTAL EST COST IN Medicare Advantage PPO			$1,695

In example 2, I wanted to see about a heart surgery. Here's what I found in the Blue Cross PPO plan document for zip code 02360. Again unconfirmed by the insurer, but in the ballpark based on their own documentation.

Table 12: Example 2—Estimated costs in a MAPD for an in-patient cardiac surgery followed by a stay in a Skilled Nursing Facility, in-network, 2025

	Cost Per Visit	# Visits	Est Cost
Pre-surgical Visits w Specialists	$45	4	$180
X-rays	$10	2	$20
MRI/CT Scan	$365	3	$1,095
Inpatient Surgery / 4 days (pay OOP for first 7 days)	$385	4	$1,540
Skilled Nursing Facility -- 30 days (1st 20 days = $0)	$170	10	$1,700
Follow Up Specialist Visits	$45	6	$270
Cardiac Rehab Program	$35	39	$1,365
TOTAL EST COST IN Medicare Advantage PPO			$6,170

Here's where costs start to really add up. In this example case, this person's costs are over $6,000. In this PPO, the in-network out-of-pocket cost maximum was $5,600. So, this person's costs were capped. But no drugs were included yet, and they would be charged separately.

To think you are getting a better deal with a MAPD may not in fact pan out over the course of your retirement. You need to do the math.

Top 10 questions to ask before choosing a MAPD

After years diving into the costs of the various Medicare options, there is no clear recipe for every person to follow. We all have preferences and perspectives. But how to decide? Do your own baking! Get in your kitchen and research your options and costs. And importantly, ask these 10 questions before signing on the dotted line for a MAPD.

Q1: Have you read the plan document for your MAPD Plan?
The long and unclear documents are readily available at each insurance company's website. Settle back and take the time to peruse nearly 300 pages. And be prepared to do this every year you are in a MAPD plan.

Q2: Are your drugs covered in the plan you want?
You cannot buy a separate standalone Part D prescription drug plan if you buy most Medicare Advantage plans. Drugs come wrapped in the package. Make sure yours are covered. Every year.

Q3: What happens if you end up in the hospital? Or need surgery?
As shown in the examples, it's almost impossible to know how much you'll pay. If you have a hospital stay, you'll front the costs for the first 4 or 5 days with a MA plan. If you have original Medicare A and B plus a Medigap, usually, you'll pay nothing for the first 60 days.

Q4: Do your doctors and specialists take your MAPD Plan?
They don't have to. You need to check before you settle on a MA plan. And every year thereafter.

Q5: If you want to switch from MAPD to Original Medicare, can you really do that?
Not really. You can quit your MAPD plan and restart your Medicare Parts A and B. However, it is unlikely you

can buy a Medigap plan without medical underwriting. Those trying to switch are generally older and sicker. They need and want more flexibility. But are most likely to be denied coverage.

In most states, insurance companies can (and do) deny access to a Medigap policy years after you started Medicare. Or they charge significantly higher rates. After all, you were the one who decided a MAPD plan was right for you.

Unless you live in Massachusetts, Connecticut, Maine, or New York, or a few other states that allow a few openings where you may be able to switch, it's unlikely you will be eligible to switch to a Medigap. (This may be changing a little starting in 2025. New laws seem to indicate there may be more flexibility to rejoin Original Medicare and buy a Medigap. We'll see...)

Q6: **How much do you like to fight with insurers?**

When you are 78, 84, 92, will you be willing to advocate for yourself if a treatment gets denied? Or a surgery gets delayed?

Remember, in a MAPD, the insurer makes the final decision. Someone who knows nothing about you decides if you can have that surgery or not. That's what preauthorization is all about.

But you can appeal the decision. Really? When you are old and sick? Seems like a tall order to me.

Q7: **Are you willing to fight for your doctor's Rx recommendation?**

MAPD private insurers place hurdles in front of a lot of specialty drugs. While you want to get better, the insurer wants cost savings. You should plan to jump through hoops to get many prescriptions if you end up with chronic diseases.

Q8: Will you have enough money to pay for expertise outside the network?

HMO members get their care inside a local network. They choose a Primary Care Physician who will make all referrals to specialists in the network.

If you would rather go outside this network, you'll need to write a big check. Healthcare professionals outside your network are under no obligation to see you. And your HMO will not cover the costs. This one's on you.

If you have a PPO, you may go out-of-network. But you'll need to get approval from the specialist you want to see. And you'll pay more.

Q9: Can MAPDs be canceled?

Yes. And you'll only have 60 days to get into a new plan. Keep in mind, the new plan may not cover all your prescriptions. And your doctors, specialists, or hospital may not be part of the new network.

Sadly, this health insurance situation can happen at any time. Even when you're 82, 92, or 102. Buyer beware.

Q10: How much should you set aside if you get really sick?

As you saw in the examples, getting sick or injured can come with a hefty price tag. Cancer treatments, dialysis, and other treatments for chronic illness can run up to the out-of-pocket maximum for several years in a row.

It's probably a good idea to create a reserve "bucket" of cash to pay these out-of-pocket maximums. If you have a Health Savings Account, HSA, that might be the answer. Or if you have millions already saved for retirement, you're probably fine.

CREATING YOUR MEDICARE RECIPE

SECTION 3:

START BAKING EARLIER THAN YOU THINK— WHEN TO ENROLL IN EACH PART OF MEDICARE

CREATING YOUR MEDICARE RECIPE

CHAPTER 10

When, Where, and How to Sign Up for Medicare Part A and Part B

Figuring out when to start each Medicare ingredient is just about the most important part of this entire process. It is much like figuring out when to take your chocolate chip cookies out of the oven. Take them out too early and they're raw in the middle. Take them out too late and they're burned.

Sure, it seems easy enough to follow the instructions in the recipe. If you're baking them at 375 degrees, it should take 11 to 13 minutes. However, if you live in a high-altitude area, you'll have to adjust the temperature, decrease the amount of baking time, change the amount of baking soda, flour, eggs, and liquid. Basically, you need a different recipe to be successful.

The recipe gives a general guideline. But you provide the custom timing based on your situation and altitude.

Automatic enrollment vs. proactive enrollment
When it comes to Medicare, the general instructions are quite easy. You simply need to be approaching your 65th birthday month, and

1. If you have been collecting Social Security for at least four months (whether receiving your own benefit before Full Retirement Age, early spousal or ex-spousal benefits, or early surviving spouse or surviving ex-spouse

benefits) you will be automatically enrolled in Medicare Part A and Part B. Both parts will start effective the first day of the month containing your 65th birthday.

- You'll receive a Welcome Kit from Medicare about two months before your birthday month with your Medicare card.
- If your birthday falls on the 1st of a month, your Part A and Part B effective date is the month before your birthday month.
- You do not have to do anything to enroll in Parts A and B.
- Your Part B monthly premium and any IRMAA will be automatically deducted from your Social Security benefits.

2. **If you are not yet collecting Social Security and will not be covered under a large employer group health plan,** you must proactively enroll in Medicare Parts A and B. But when exactly will you proactively enroll?

The Initial Enrollment Period—your IEP

The technical rule is that someone who has not yet claimed Social Security and who does not have large group health insurance coverage has seven months to enroll in Parts A and B. This is called the Initial Enrollment Period, or IEP.

Those who are on an ACA Marketplace plan as they reach age 65 need to enroll in Medicare during their IEP as will those on COBRA and most "retiree" health insurance plans.

The IEP is anchored on the month containing your 65th birthday. You can apply three months before your 65th birthday month, the month of your birthday, and up to three months after your 65th birthday month.

When applying the months before your birthday month, Medicare A and B start the first day of your 65th birthday month. When applying during your birthday month or after, your insurance starts the first day of the following month.

It's critical you don't leave any months open where you have no health insurance. The best practice is to apply for both Medicare Parts A and B three months before your 65th birthday month. That way, your coverage will begin the first day of the month containing your 65th birthday.

For example, if your birthday is March 10th, you want to apply for Parts A and B the first week in December of the prior year.

There's one catch: If your birthday falls on the first day of the month, your IEP starts four months before your 65th birthday month and extends to two months after. So if your birthday is March 1st, you need your Medicare Parts A and B to start on February 1st. Therefore, you'll apply the first week of the prior November.

And this is the easy enrollment option!

Hold on, we're not done with the proactive enrollment rules... There's a lot more to know about your personal situation before applying during your IEP. Lots of older workers do not need to jump in so early. You need to consider your employment situation, your spouse's or partner's employment situation, and when you are going to claim Social Security.

There are different rules for joining Part A and Part B based on the size of your employer, other options you may have for insurance, whether you are an active or inactive employee, or if it's economical to remain in your employer's plan. Your marital status also matters. As does your participating in a Health Savings Account (HSA), and if you are contributing to it.

When to sign up for Medicare A and B is a complex web of rules. Each person needs to figure out their correct timing. For example:

- If you are older than 65 and no longer actively working at a large company (20 or more employees), you need to apply three months before you retire or leave the employer plan. Coordinate your last day of the group plan at work with your first day on Medicare.

- If you are older than 65 and no longer going to be covered on your spouse's large group employer health insurance plan, apply for Parts A and B three months before you lose group coverage.

- If you continue working for a small employer (fewer than 20 employees) after age 65, you must proactively sign up for Parts A and B—ideally, three months before your 65th birthday month. You may also need Part D and Medigap. Apply one month before your 65th birthday month for those two plans.

- If you are nearing age 70 and continuing to work for a large employer, you'll want to sign up for Social Security the month or two before your 70th birthday month. Medicare Part A will automatically be turned on, but you can delay Part B until you stop working or lose large group health insurance.

- If you are the domestic partner and are covered by the other partner's large employer group plan, it is highly likely you need to enroll in Parts A and B during your IEP. Most large plans do not cover partners after age 65, except as secondary payers. You'll need Parts A and B in place by age 65 to cover the majority of your expenses.

What's with these overly complicated instructions?
You must be thinking, good grief, we're not making a choco-

late souffle here. Just some basic chocolate chip cookies. After all, virtually everyone 65 and older needs to get on Medicare. What's with all these timing rules? And, what if I don't sign up on time?

Simply put, if you don't get Medicare right, you are stuck paying for your own medical care. And very likely, you will pay a permanent penalty on your Part B premium for your entire retirement. Yowza.

Medicare was not always this complicated. Back in 1965, there was one set of rules for most people. Sign up for Social Security (this is not a typo) at 65—the mandatory retirement age at most companies.

When you signed up for Social Security at 65, Medicare Parts A and B started automatically. So, you were all set starting the month of your 65th birthday. The most complicated situation was for those whose birthdays fell on the first day of the month.

That was it. Plain vanilla, you might say.

Baby Boomers didn't want to retire at 65
But a funny thing happened when those first Baby Boomers started turning 65. Many of them didn't want to retire. Some had great jobs, loved working, and wanted to continue to make a difference. Others didn't feel they could comfortably afford to retire.

So, the Boomers made a big deal about forced retirement. Congress eventually passed four critical laws that today, shape our highly complex landscape for working longer, receiving benefits, and dealing with Medicare:

- **Federal Age Discrimination in Employment Act of 1967.** This law prohibits a mandatory retirement age for most jobs and protects those 40 and older from indiscriminate termination. However, it didn't require employers to provide benefits. If they offered health insurance to older employees, they could be charged more.

- **Older Workers Benefit Protection Act of 1990.** This law addressed the benefits problem by specifying workers 65 and older could not be discriminated against in any employee benefits.

- **Medicare Secondary Payer Provisions of the Social Security Act, 1980.** This amendment prohibits Medicare from paying claims if an employer is a primary payer. Small business health plans (fewer than 20 employees) are not considered primary payers for those 65 and older.

- **Senior Citizens' Freedom to Work Act of 2000.** This law repealed the Social Security earnings limit test for those who reached Full Retirement Age (FRA) and continued to work. When working after FRA and claiming Social Security, any earnings would offset Social Security benefits. When the worker's benefit is not paid, any dependents also lose their benefits.

The combination of these law changes meant Baby Boomers could continue to stay employed, **and** get employer-sponsored health insurance at the same price as younger workers, **and** receive their full Social Security benefits once they reached FRA.

Phew! That took some time and a whole lot of action in Congress to straighten up the situation for older workers. But it's also why getting into Medicare takes on a life of its own.

Working after 65 and your health insurance

Now that we can all work beyond 65, what do we do about Medicare? There is a well-known penalty if you do not enroll in Medicare at 65. And it's permanent. Well, that's not exactly correct.

The law is actually more complex (of course). You will pay a penalty on your Medicare Part B premiums if you fail to enroll *on time*. Determining your individual enrollment time depends on your age and your employment situation and your Social Security claiming decisions.

Furthermore, the size of the employer matters. If you are working for a large company, defined for Medicare purposes as one with 20 or more employees, there is one set of rules. If you work for a company with fewer than 20 employees, there is another set of rules. And, if you are not an "active" employee, you have completely different rules to follow.

In addition, if you are a spouse and receive your health insurance from your spouse's employer plan, you are generally covered under their large employer plan. But if you are a domestic partner who gets health insurance from your partner, federal law currently does not allow the large employer group plan to pay primary for your healthcare claims.

Let's look in more detail at a few different situations...

Worker, 65+, enrolled in a large group health plan, no Social Security yet
If you are 65 or older, actively working for a large company, enrolled in the employer's health insurance plan, and have not claimed Social Security, you do not need to enroll in any part of Medicare. Not Part A. Not Part B. Certainly not a Medigap or Medicare Advantage. And not Part D if you also have creditable drug coverage.

If you are fully enrolled in your group plan and remain in the plan, you have complete health insurance.

However, many people will enroll in Part A if they are eligible for premium-free Part A. This can be a good idea, but only if you are not contributing to a Health Savings Account (HSA).

Once you have any part of Medicare, contributions to the tax-favored HSAs are no longer allowed. And, in fact, HSA contributions are not allowed 6-to-9-months retroactively to Part A, or back to age 65, whichever is shorter, based on when you apply for Part A.

When you are getting ready to retire or leave the employer group health plan, you will want to proactively apply for your full Medicare insurance and ensure it is in place first.

Worker, 65+, enrolled in a large group health plan, claimed Social Security

If someone is 65 or older, actively working for a large company, enrolled in the employer's health insurance plan, and has already claimed Social Security, they may be surprised to receive their Medicare card in the mail.

Claiming Social Security after age 65 automatically starts Medicare Part A. You cannot decouple Part A from Social Security. Part B also automatically starts if you aren't careful.

This is a common situation for someone who is working after age 70. When they reach age 70, they should have claimed their maximum Social Security benefit. The application for Social Security also triggered Part A to start retroactively and may have kicked on Part B.

But if the worker continues to be covered by a large employer group plan, they can delay Part B. Do not select Part B on the application. Or follow the specific steps in the "Welcome to Medicare" packet that comes in the mail. You must return the Medicare card to postpone Part B within 60 days.

Later, when retiring or leaving the employer group health plan, apply just for Medicare Part B.

For many older workers, it is not a problem to have Part A turned on. However, if they have a Health Savings Account (HSA), contributions to these tax-favored accounts are no longer allowed. HSA contributions were not allowed 6-to-9-months retroactively to Part A's effective date, or back to age 65, whichever is shorter, based on when you applied for Social Security.

A typical example: A worker turning 70 on July 27th is ready to claim Social Security. They apply in May. Their Part A starts retroactively as soon as their Social Security application is submitted. So, Part A started the prior November. And the last HSA contribution should have been the prior October.

Worker, 65+, enrolled in a small employer health plan, no Social Security yet
If you are reaching age 65, working for a small company or if you are the owner of a small business (fewer than 20 employees), different Medicare rules will apply. If you are enrolled in the company's health insurance plan and have not claimed Social Security, you **must proactively enroll** in Medicare Parts A and B during the three months before your 65th birthday month. Even though the small company health insurance is still available to you. This is critical to get right.

- You must enroll in Parts A and B so you will have primary coverage for any hospital or physician bills you'll incur while working.

- Your spouse or partner who is turning 65 must enroll in both Parts A and B before their 65th birthday month for continuous coverage.

If you haven't signed up in the three months before your 65th birthday month, you effectively have no insurance at all. Small business health insurance plans cannot pay as a primary insurer.

Medicare Part A's inconvenient "6-month" retroactive period is really 9-months
As you can see, it is relatively easy to run afoul of Medicare rules. Especially when it comes to getting enrollment just right

when working after age 65. There seem to be an unending number of hidden rules and traps. One of the worst is this one: Unbeknownst to you, your Medicare Part A—but NOT your Medicare Part B—begins retroactively either back to the month of your 65th birthday or 6-months before your *application date* for either Social Security or Medicare.

Say what?

I know, it's a crazy thing. It has nothing to do with you, and everything to do with who is going to pay your claims during this "limbo" period before leaving your employer's group plan. The basic premise here is that no one wants to pay hospitalization charges. Neither your employer nor the insurance company want to pay the bills when you really could be in Medicare after age 65. But by law, the employer's plan must cover older workers as the primary payer.

So, it was decided that for those employees who work after age 65 for a large employer, Medicare will cover the costs of hospitalizations and other Part A needs retroactively. That way, the employer and its insurer don't take on the full additional risks for older workers as they transition into Medicare.

You will see an unexpected Part A effective date on your Medicare card. When you apply for Social Security or Medicare Part A after 65, the Part A effective date is six months before the **application date**. When most workers retire after age 65, Part A started nine months before their retirement date.

No one ever tells employees this little piece of news. And frankly, it doesn't matter to you who pays your Part A bills… so long as it's not you. Except in the case where you also have an HSA you are funding.

Fixing HSA excess contributions
Unknowingly, before joining Medicare Part A you may have

contributed too much to your HSA. If your employer also made a contribution, they may have made an ineligible contribution as well. And the problem to fix it falls in your lap.

You will need to remove excess contributions. If you discover the excess contributions before your tax filing deadline, work with your HR group or the payroll people to pull out the excess and create a corrected W-2. If you've crossed a tax year, you'll need to work with your tax professional to amend your tax returns from earlier years.

Hard to know those rules when no one is telling you. There is no one coordinating between Part A's retroactive rules and HSA contributions. It's simply a problem taxpayers have to struggle with when they are surprised during tax season.

TIP: Use IRS Publication 969 for HSA rules. And refer to the instructions for IRS Form 8889 for details on which months allow eligible HSA contributions.

The Part B SEP: Special Enrollment Period
Many older workers are still concerned about getting a Part B penalty for late entry into Medicare. Be assured you will not get hit with a penalty for late enrollment if you are continuously covered by a large employer group health insurance plan. You or your spouse must be enrolled in the plan to be covered.

There is an additional piece of the Medicare law that allows those 65+ to join Medicare Part B after their Initial Enrollment Period is long gone. It's called the SEP, or Special Enrollment Period, and is specifically designed to accommodate older workers who stayed on a large employer's group health insurance plan.

Simply put, the SEP allows you to enroll "on time" into Medicare Part B. Where you would normally enroll around your 65th birthday month, your large group plan was providing your insurance in lieu of Part B. Only when you are getting ready to leave this employer and the group plan will you need to get your Part B in place.

Technically, the SEP allows you eight months *after* you leave the large group plan to start your Part B. But do not use these eight months! The SEP only provides you access to enter Part B outside of your IEP without incurring a penalty. But you have no primary health insurance during that period.

The bottom line is, so long as you have been continuously covered by a large employer's group health insurance plan since you turned 65, you are fine. You apply for Medicare three months before ending your employment. No, you cannot choose COBRA. No, you cannot use "retiree" health insurance. No, you cannot hop on the ACA Marketplace plans. None of those options pay as a primary insurer after age 65. Run from them as fast and as far as you can. They are a younger-person's continuity of insurance provision.

The SEP is particularly helpful if you have an unplanned situation after turning 65 such as losing your job or getting unexpectedly sick. You'll need to quickly get yourself enrolled in Medicare so you can limit your time without primary health insurance. And avoid the Part B penalty.

The Part B General Enrollment Period
You can join Medicare Part A anytime after age 65. But Part B has restrictions on when you can join. You can only enroll during your IEP or if you qualify for an off-cycle SEP. If you've missed both, there is one more chance: the General Enrollment Period, or GEP. This opening allows you to enroll in Part B in the first quarter of the year. January, February, and March are the only months you can enroll in Part B if you've made a mistake and don't have it in place on time.

The GEP is open each year to allow retirees into this part of Medicare. This is the time when penalties usually apply. For those who make mistakes, or didn't want Medicare early in retirement but who are now ill, the door is still open. But you'll likely be assessed the Part B penalty. You'll pay an extra 10% per year you missed being enrolled in Part B. And it's a permanent penalty.

So, if someone didn't want Part B—*"I've never seen a doctor my entire life!"*—but now needs medical attention and help paying high costs, they can still get in. That's the good news. But, if they are 70 years old, they will be assessed a 50% penalty for the five years they've not had Part B. This is a permanent penalty that gets recalculated every year.

An example: If someone is 70 in January 2025, didn't enroll in Part B at age 65, and was not covered by a large employer group plan, the penalty will apply. It is calculated by Social Security as follows:

Standard, or base, premium = $185/month
50% late entry penalty = $185 x .5 = $92.50/month
New Part B premium = $185 + $92.50 = $277.50/month

That's an extra $1,110 this person will pay for their Part B. If they also have higher income and are subject to IRMAA, it will be tacked on to the new, higher Part B premium.

Assume the standard premium increases each year. The 50% penalty will be applied to the new standard premium. This is repeated every year in retirement. A permanent penalty.

Some people have asked if they can appeal the penalty. Sure, you can appeal anything you are unhappy with. But you likely won't win this appeal. At this time, only if you had Part B in place during at least some of the time period, or you had some large-employer health insurance coverage, would you have a shot at an adjustment. The mere fact that you didn't know about the "on time" enrollment rules does not get you out of the penalty.

Like burnt cookies. You can't unburn them.

Special notes for married couples and partners
One of the biggest adjustments when making the transition to Medicare is that Medicare is truly an individual plan. After forty-something years when one spouse's health insurance plan covered the entire family, that option disappears overnight. The impact starts when the older spouse turns 65.

That spouse will navigate Medicare first and figure out their best combination of coverage. The younger spouse is then on their own. They will need to assess the various options available to them and get ready to make a pre-Medicare transition.

The options available to the younger spouse vary by your household situation. Here are a handful of possibilities that could apply to you:

- ACA Marketplace in your state.
- COBRA continuation insurance if the holder of the insurance is leaving employment.
- Private health insurance plans (this is typically the only option if you do not qualify for the Advanced Premium Tax Credit).
- Tricare if you are part of a qualifying military family.
- Union health insurance plans that allow a spouse or partner to remain in the plan.
- Federal Employee benefits for federal government workers and spouses.

You may have other options due to your personal situation, but these are some common ones.

It is a good idea to find a strong, unbiased consumer advocate who can help you identify all your choices and navigate the ACA plans in your area. Or you might look for an independent insurance broker who is trained to help sort through the bronze, silver, and gold plans. Using the federal government's healthcare website will help you figure out the ACA system in your state. Start at Healthcare.gov, then find your state and zip code.

If you cover anyone else, such as a minor child, an adult child under age 26, or a disabled person, they also lose coverage from your group plan when you roll into Medicare. They'll have other options available for health insurance coverage. You'll need to explore your state's options on the ACA Marketplace, with Medicaid, the CHIP program, and any other options you may have.

Additional notes for the active worker: If you, the worker, is 62, for example, and your spouse is 78, your spouse can still be covered by the large group plan, as long as spouses are otherwise covered by the plan. The older spouse should have claimed Social Security by age 70, so they have Medicare Part A. But there is no need to have Medicare Part B and pay Part B premiums at this time.

Where and how to enroll in Medicare Part A and Part B
Learning the ins and outs of Medicare during the transition stage is the tricky part. There is a tremendous amount of new information flying from all directions. But, fortunately, when it comes to enrolling in Medicare, it is relatively easy.

The most efficient way to apply is online. Your first stop is Social Security's website. Yes, you find the application for Medicare Parts A and B on SSA.gov. If you go to Medicare.gov and try to enroll, the link sends you to SSA.gov.

Look for the link or icon for applying for benefits. Today, there is an option to "sign up for Medicare." In the various formats of SSA's website, things will move or slightly change names. But the option to sign up for Medicare will be fairly obvious.

CREATING YOUR MEDICARE RECIPE

You will be directed to your online *mySocialSecurity* account. Make sure to have your username and password handy.

- If you don't have a *mySocialSecurity* account, you will be prompted to set one up first. This is a critical step to keep you information secure.
- You'll find your most current Social Security statement and benefits estimate behind the login, as well as your Medicare Part A status.

Once you are in the application system, you can apply for any of the following:

- **Both Medicare Parts A and B**—This is the option you'll choose if you apply during your IEP, no longer have large employer group health insurance, or are turning 65 and have an ACA Marketplace plan or private insurance.
- **Just Medicare Part A**—If you continue working at a large employer that provides health insurance, and you are enrolled in that plan, you do not need to enroll in any part of Medicare. But many people want to get their premium-free Part A in place. That's fine if you do not have an HSA or don't want to continue to contribute to your HSA.
- **Early Social Security benefits plus Medicare Part A**—If you need to claim Social Security retirement benefits early, you can do so. Medicare Part A will automatically start at age 65 even if you have health insurance at work. Keep in mind, you will be locking in a permanently reduced Social Security benefit when claiming early. Your monthly income may be significantly lower than if you wait until your Full Retirement Age. As much as 30% lower if you claim at age 62 as a worker and 35% lower if you claim as a dependent spouse.
- **Early Social Security benefits plus Medicare Parts A and B**— If you need full Medicare coverage at 65 and want to claim Social Security at the same time, you can apply for both.

When, Where, and How to Sign Up for Medicare Part A and Part B

If you apply only for Part A, you will come back to your account on SSA.gov months or years later to add Part B. The process will be similar: log in to your account, choose the "sign up for Medicare" option, and then the "enroll in Part B only" link. You enter your Medicare number from your Medicare card to start the Part B application.

You will need to provide additional information during the online application or after Social Security receives your application:

- Proof from your employer that you have been covered by group health insurance continuously since you turned 65.
- The form needed is the CMS L-564. You can download it online or check with your employer if they prefer to send you a form.
- You and your employer each fill out one section and sign. If you are covering a spouse, they need their own form.
- Request the form before starting the Medicare application. You'll want a PDF to upload. And a printed copy if you are going to a local Social Security office.

If you don't care for online applications or haven't been able to set up your mySocialSecurity account, you can make a phone appointment or an in-person appointment with Social Security. Plan to wait a long time on hold just to make the appointment. Securing an in-person appointment is not available at every field office.

Signing up for Medicare is simple to do online. But if you have a complex situation, speaking with a Social Security agent may be necessary.

A few tips for using the online application:

- As of this writing, use Chrome as your browser.
- The application is not completely intuitive in some parts.

If you are applying for both Part A and Part B at the same time, there is nowhere to check a box for Part A. Rather, the assumption is you are applying for Part A. Social Security just needs to know if you are also applying for Part B. There's a check box for that.

- You'll see a "Remarks" box midway through the form. Use that box to let Social Security know exactly when you'd like to start your Part B. Ideally, your start date will be three months after you apply.
- Write down your re-entry number if you don't complete the application in one sitting.
- Print all confirmations and keep for your records.
- Look for mail from Social Security. They will communicate with you through the regular mail and will let you know your application has been received, if they need any other information, and how much your Part B premium will be. Any IRMAA upcharges will be sent in a separate letter.

CHAPTER 11

When, How, and Where to Sign Up for Medicare Part D or a MAPD

Getting the timing just right in your Medicare recipe also includes knowing exactly when to sign up for your prescription drug coverage. There are different penalties if you don't get your standalone Part D or prescription coverage in a Medicare Advantage plan (MAPD) at the right time.

But before you sign up for the one plan that will work for you, you need to do a lot of shopping. You'll need to check several grocery stores to see if they carry your exact ingredients. Some will, but others may only carry a few of your ingredients (specific drugs).

Plan to spend at least a few hours shopping for your Part D or MAPD. And visit several insurance companies' websites (stores).

Signing up for Medicare Part D the first time
It would seem logical that you would sign up for Medicare Part D on SSA.gov along with Parts A and B. But logic is not part of this process. In fact, you will not use any government site to sign up for Part D.

Instead, you'll start with the Medicare "find plans" tool on Medicare.gov. This is where you research and shop for your Part D options. This tool is similar to Expedia.com or VRBO.

com or any other aggregating online application. It is a powerful tool where you'll see all the insurance providers that cover your specific drugs in your zip code and county. Costs for your Rx's are shown along with the Part D monthly premium and the drug deductible. But only for the remaining months of the year.

Since Part D plans or MAPDs can only cover your prescriptions starting with the first day of the month following your application, you will only see costs for a partial year. Unless you are shopping during the Open Enrollment Period (OEP) between October 15 and December 7, or if you are shopping in December. Then you'll see the full cost for the following year.

This is particularly important for your budget planning when you're entering a Part D plan for the first time mid-year. You may think your costs will be, say $500. Then you're surprised the following year when costs are $1,000. Plan carefully.

Contact the Part D insurance company directly
Once you find a drug plan that works for you, and it is the least expensive overall plan, you'll contact the corresponding insurance company directly. You can link to their website from Medicare's "find plans" tool and sign up online or call the 800 number.

I recommend calling the Part D insurance company to confirm the current prices of each of your drugs. Some people get one price in the "find plans" tool, sign up for that Part D plan, and then get charged a higher price. That's because the insurers can change the price of prescriptions throughout the year.

So, call the 800 number and ask about prices and how you will be notified if there is a price change.

Signing up for Part D is a completely separate process from signing up for Medicare Parts A and B. You must have your

When, How, and Where to Sign Up for Medicare Part D or a MAPD

Medicare number already in place before you can buy a Part D plan. You can have Part A in place, Part B in place, or both. But you need one part of Medicare for Part D to "snap onto."

You'll want to call the Part D insurer you chose one month prior to your Medicare start date. Generally, you want to coordinate all pieces and parts of Medicare to start on the same day. There may be some exceptions if you are still on a creditable drug plan at your employer. But most often, individuals get fully into Medicare at one time.

Let's say June 1st is your Medicare target date. You'll call the Part D insurance company the first week in May to apply and to confirm your drug coverage and costs. Your plan will become effective on June 1st. You'll also set up a payment plan with the insurer to make sure you don't miss any monthly premium payments.

Your Part D card will arrive in the mail with a number on it. Notify your doctors and anyone who prescribes your drugs. They will now need to bill that insurance company and send your Rx requests to the new pharmacy or mail order house.

If you are having trouble finding a Part D plan that covers one of your Rx's or the price for a prescription is too expensive for your budget, contact your SHIP organization for assistance. You can find your local group at https://www.shiphelp.org/ .

Choosing a Medicare Advantage plan with drug coverage
If you decide a MAPD is the way to go, you'll want to make sure the plan you choose covers all your prescription drugs.

Important note: if you choose a MAPD, you cannot buy a standalone Part D plan. Those two simply don't mix, like oil and water. You may see a few Medicare Advantage plans offered in your zip code without drug plans. They are sometime offered in Private-Fee-for-Service plans or Medical Savings Account plans. It is rare that people choose these plans.

The intent of the packaged MAPD is for you to get your complete Medicare coverage under the same plan without outside options. In fact, if you buy a MAPD-HMO or MAPD-PPO, and also buy a standalone drug plan, you will be kicked out of the MAPD plan.

You will typically apply for the MAPD choice that fits your situation when first enrolling in Medicare. It may be during your IEP or during a SEP. You must enroll in Medicare Parts A and B first before applying for a MAPD. As soon as you have your Medicare number, you'll want to contact the MAPD insurance company to enroll in your plan.

Once you have Part B in place, you have 63 days to enroll in a Medicare Advantage plan to get your prescription drug coverage on time and without penalties.

If you didn't coordinate signing up for Part B with your MAPD, there is only one other time each year to buy a MAPD as a first-timer. This is the annual Open Enrollment Period that runs from October 15 to December 7. You can buy a MAPD at that time and coverage begins on January first.

The Part D penalty
Most people do not pay a premium to Medicare to have a Part D plan. They do pay a monthly premium to the Part D insurer. In addition, high income folks do pay IRMAA upcharges to Medicare. However, if you fail to get into a Part D plan on time, you will find yourself in the penalty box. For your entire retirement. Ouch!

The Part D penalty is assessed on a monthly basis. If you miss your entry, you will be assessed a 1% per month penalty for the number of months you were without a plan. So, if you should have started your Part D on January 1, 2021, and are just joining now during OEP, your Part D will begin on January 1, 2025. And you missed 48 months being in a Part D plan.

Your penalty will be calculated as 48% of the national base beneficiary premium for drug plans. In 2025 that premium is $36.78. You would, therefore, pay your standalone Part D insurer o their monthly premium plus $17.70 per month in penalty charges.

After the initial penalty is set, the Part D insurer will recalculate it each subsequent year. The base beneficiary premium will change each year, likely increasing. And you'll be stuck paying extra for your entire retirement.

Reshopping during annual Open Enrollment Period
Your Part D plans are a "1-year contract." Everything can change from year to year. It's up to you to reshop your plans. While you initially enroll in Part D only once, you will reshop for 30 years, give or take.

I recommend putting a permanent to-do on your calendar for every November 1st. Get this necessary baking done before Thanksgiving. You'll know before the holidays that your optimal drug plan is in place for the following year.

If you want to later switch to a MAPD or change your plan
Some retirees start out with Medicare Parts A and B, a Medigap plan, and a standalone Part D. Later, they decide to switch to a MAPD. They can do so during the annual OEP, October 15 thru December 7. The new MAPD will start on January 1.

Other retirees start with one MAPD then want to switch to another insurer's MAPD or another type of MAPD at their current insurance company—such as switching from an HMO to a PPO. Those changes are available also during the Open Enrollment Period.

Those with a MAPD can also switch to Original Medicare Parts A and B during OEP. But always check if you can still get a Medigap plan before dropping your MAPD. And find a standalone Part D plan that covers your Rx's.

To make a switch, call the 800 number at the insurance company where you want your new plan. They will give you any instructions for joining the new plan and disenrolling in the old. Follow them carefully. You will generally be disenrolled from your current MAPD and enrolled in the new plan automatically.

You have one other time to change a MAPD if you already have one. This is the Medicare Advantage Open Enrollment Period. It runs from January 1– March 31 each year. You'll be able to switch to another MAPD or drop your current MAPD and join Original Medicare plus add a Part D drug plan. Remember, though, you may not be able to get into a Medigap plan if you switch to Original Medicare. The new plan starts the first day of the month following the application.

High degree of plan management

It can be challenging for many older Americans to deal with changing their Part D prescription drug plan every year. But that is, in fact, what each person needs to do every year in Medicare. Each Part D plan is only a 12-month contract. You need to reshop every year to see if it's still the best plan to cover your prescriptions. Or if a new Part D plan is better.

It's even more challenging to deal with managing your plan when you go the MAPD route. It is so important to understand how involved you'll need to be. There are many reasons why your particular MAPD can change every year. There can be changes to your Rx's, your favorite doctor may no longer accept the plan, or the plan reduced its extra goodies offered.

It is up to you to read your Annual Notice of Changes (ANOC) and Explanation of Coverage (EOC). These legal documents help you stay on top of changes. You'll only have about seven weeks to shop around for a new plan every year...even when you're in your 80s and 90s and beyond.

CHAPTER 12

Ingredients That Do Not Belong in Your Medicare Recipe

As most bakers know, you can have a lot of fun experimenting with all kinds of ingredients to create something unexpectedly delicious. The chocolate chip cookie itself was a result of trying a new ingredient when in a pinch.

But bakers also know that some things just don't go together. You would not add hamburger to your chocolate chip cookie batter, for example. Or chopped celery. There is a limit to pushing the baking envelope.

And there is a limit on ingredients in your personal Medicare recipe. There are other health insurance plans that interfere with your Medicare planning. It's as important you know what you can't have in your Medicare grocery bag as what you need to have.

COBRA and "Retiree" insurance are really for younger folks
One of the most frustrating parts of getting Medicare right is trying to understand what an employer's plan documents say, and what they mean. There is nothing wrong with the documents, except no one understands them. The most egregious areas are regarding COBRA and "retiree" insurance. These are two transition plans available when you are losing group coverage. And in practical reality, they are almost always only for those under 65.

Understand the default position is that Medicare pays primary (pays claims first and most) once someone reaches age 65. The only exception is if the person is an actively working employee for a large company. Active employment means you are doing the 9:00 to 5:00 thing and receiving a paycheck from a large employer. Or your spouse is working, and their company plan ordinarily allows coverage for spouses.

When the person who carries the health insurance is leaving the large group plan, they are offered an option to continue the insurance under COBRA—the Consolidated Omnibus Budget Reconciliation Act of 1986. Some companies also offer "retiree" insurance where you can remain in the group plan. You may have to pay a higher or the full premium.

Unfortunately, as active workers become formerly active workers, it appears they can sign up for COBRA. If the former employee is 65 or older, the COBRA option is generally off the table. And most "retiree" insurance ends at 65 as well. Many HR folks tell the exiting worker they can be covered on the group health plan for another 18 months. That is simply not the case for those 65 and older. It is true, however, if the worker leaving the plan is under 65.

Other insurance pays secondary to Medicare Parts A and B
Technically, you can buy the continuation coverage offered at your employer. It's expensive and usually won't pay your insurance claims. COBRA and retiree plans offered to former employees over age 65 pay secondary to Medicare. If Medicare Parts A and B are not in place, there is nothing to pay secondary to. Furthermore, once the insurance company figures out (and they often do) they paid a claim for a 65+ person, they can reverse that payment.

And you, the former worker, are on the hook for paying the bill.

The big take-away here is that you need to know that COBRA and "retiree" insurance are truly designed to protect you and your family members when you are younger than 65. This way you are not uncovered between jobs. Or a younger spouse or partner can have some time to find other insurance when you leave your job and join Medicare. In those cases, the transitional insurance pays primary.

TIP: Avoid this problem. Just get yourself into Medicare before you leave your job when you are 65 and older!

The ACA Marketplace plans don't work after 65

Another area of health insurance wreaking havoc for some is the transition off ACA Marketplace plans as they reach age 65. On the one hand, we are grateful to have this option for health insurance when an employer doesn't offer health insurance or when COBRA runs out after 18 months (generally the length of time someone younger than 65 can continue health insurance after losing a job). On the other hand, the details about what happens when you turn 65 are buried in the bowels of the plan footnotes.

The health insurance plans we're used to only apply to those who have not yet reached their 65th birthday month. Once the first day of the month containing your 65th birthday rolls around, you are in Medicare land. No other health insurance will pay your claims. Except if you are that active employee in a large group plan. Or the spouse of an active employee.

So, it should be no surprise that the ACA plans work the same way. They are for younger folks. But it is not clear that this is the case. You do **not** get a notice that your ACA plan should be ending. When you don't magically know this, not only will your primary healthcare costs not get paid by the insurer, but you will also lose your Advanced Premium Tax Credit and may have to pay back some of the credits received.

CREATING YOUR MEDICARE RECIPE

If you thought you'd wait till the end of the year before hopping into Medicare, forget it. You also have to magically know to enroll in Medicare the three months before turning 65 so you have continuous primary coverage and no gaps once your 65th birthday month rolls around.

TIP: Make sure you keep track of your Medicare Initial Enrollment Period. You own the transition from ACA Marketplace plans to Medicare. It's up to you to enroll on time to avoid Part B and Part D penalties.

SECTION 4:

CHECKING YOUR PANTRY FOR MORE—OPTIONAL INGREDIENTS, IMPORTANT INFORMATION, RESOURCES

CHAPTER 13

Dental, Vision, Hearing Coverage— Do You Really Need Them?

One might argue that eating three handfuls of chocolate chips while baking cookies is not ideal. Others would disagree. Some recommend adding butterscotch chips in with the chocolate chips for their cookies. Others want to stick with the original.

That's the same idea deciding if you want a cost-sharing solution for dental, vision, and hearing services—those parts of healthcare specifically excluded from the Medicare law. Even though older Americans need these services more than others.

What happened in Congress in 1965?
When the Medicare law finally passed after 20 years of debate in Congress, it stayed focused on the areas causing the most difficulty for seniors. Namely, paying for hospitalization and skilled nursing care, and ensuring payments to doctors. The law specifically carved out cost help for dental, vision, and hearing. It also left out coverage for long-term care. And the original Medicare law did not cap out-of-pocket (OOP) costs. That's why you need a Medigap plan to provide protection against your OOP costs, or a Medicare Advantage plan (MAPD).

It's important to recognize there's a lot of sausage-making in Washington to get a bill over the finish line. Lots of compromise results in leaving certain provisions out and keeping others in.

Like most new bills with sweeping impact, the initial bill gets rolled out, and over time, it is adjusted and expanded. There have been plenty of adjustments to Medicare over the last 60 years. Just not to add in dental, vision, and hearing.

While there has been a renewed interest by older Americans and politicians in recent years to expand Medicare to include these missing and important coverages, it is not a universal request. When stacked up against long-term care costs, these expenses are simply not top priorities. And, frankly, even if you need expensive dental work, it's not that expensive. When nursing home care can top $160,000 per year[15] and the average stay is three years, a $15,000 dental procedure pales in comparison.

Finding coverage for dental
Even though Medicare does not cover most dental procedures—Part A covers oral surgery that requires hospitalization—you can find coverage in the private insurance market. But before you spend your money on dental plans or give up flexibility by going the Medicare Part C route, do the math. It is really worth spending $50/month on premiums ($600/year) for two dental cleanings and an x-ray?

Here's the situation: dental coverage is different from medical insurance. With a dental plan, you enter into a cost-sharing arrangement with a dollar limit. You have two insurance choices for finding dental coverage.

1. You can buy a standalone dental plan at many of the insurance companies where you'll buy a Medigap. Some Medigaps offer dental along with their plans. Or you can buy a policy from Delta Dental or AARP in most states or from a different private insurance company (Anthem, Guardian, etc.). Premiums tend to range from about $25 to $75 per person per month, depending on the level of coverage you choose. Or,

Dental, Vision, Hearing Coverage—Do You Really Need Them?

2. You can choose a Medicare Advantage plan that includes dental coverage. There is no additional premium to add dental coverage. But you are limited to a specific network of dentists or will pay a larger share of the costs if you go out-of-network.

You also have the option to pay on your own and forego an additional insurance plan and monthly premium. Talk to your dentist and see what they recommend for folks going on Medicare. Many dentists have their own discounts or memberships. Also find out if they take any of the dental plans you are considering.

Dental coverage is quite limited—plan for out-of-pocket expenses
Even if you decide to go with a dental plan, you're still going to pay for many dental needs throughout retirement. The plans are limited to a set dollar amount per year. You do get some basic benefits such as: discounts or low copays for preventive cleanings and x-rays; a set dollar amount of coverage for basic oral procedures such as fillings and non-surgical tooth extractions; and, a maximum dollar amount for major dental work like crowns, root canals, and implants.

Many dental plans have waiting periods for any major work, dentures, and implants. And the cost savings may be less than you'd like. In addition to the premium for standalone plans, you might pay $0 for two cleanings per year, 20% of the cost for basic procedures, and 50% of the cost for major dental work. Your plan will typically pay a maximum of $1,000, $1,200, or $1,500 per year. After that, you pay full freight.

The bottom line with dental: Do your homework. Talk to your dentist about costs with and without a dental plan. Make sure it is worth the monthly premiums if you don't have a lot of dental needs.

Vision plans are not what you may think
While many seniors complain they don't have vision coverage with Medicare, they also don't get much with vision plans.

Standalone vision plans are readily available in the insurance market, similar to dental plans. You can buy these cost-sharing plans at many insurance companies, along with your Medigap plan, and they come bundled with most MAPDs. VSP and AARP are two popular options for vision plans. Premiums for standalone plans tend to run between $15 and $30 per person per month in 2025.

But be prepared to pay a lot out-of-pocket. Vision plans typically only pay for one vision exam per year after you pay a small copay around $15 to $25. Then you'll get $100 or $200 toward glasses or contacts every one or two years.

Is saving $100 going to make a dent in the cost of your glasses? Two or three pairs of glasses can cost $500 to $1,200 or more. Overall, you might come out a little ahead with a vision plan, but the savings is in the eye exam visit. You might pay about $200 for the exam without the vision plan, and $20 with the plan + $120 for the premium.

Again, this is a situation that requires some research and homework on your part. First call is to your eye doctor to ask about options and recommendations. Because vision plans are part of networks, you'll want to know which plans your doctor participates in. Also check which plans your favorite eyeglasses place accepts. Take your time and consider the options you have in your area.

If you're thinking vision plans may be necessary or at least helpful, run the numbers. And make sure you give yourself the flexibility you need to see the doctor of your choice.

What about coverage for hearing tests and hearing aids?
It won't surprise you at this point that you'll find the same kinds of cost-sharing coverage for hearing aids—very little coverage for an expensive and necessary device.

Most hearing aids cost between $1,000 and $3,500 per ear.

Dental, Vision, Hearing Coverage—Do You Really Need Them?

So, you're looking at a price tag that can easily reach $7,500 or more. Some over-the-counter options start at $99 per pair. Hearing aids generally have a life of three to five years. Get your first pair at age 65, and you'll likely buy another six pairs during retirement.

The prices vary dramatically depending on different variables, technology support, and your hearing needs. The new technology of integrating your hearing aids with your smart phone is pretty impressive.

Getting help paying for hearing aids is not so simple. AARP has a discount plan with a single hearing aid starting at $699 and additional discounts available. You'll need to be an AARP member, but you do not need to have United Healthcare as your Medigap provider.

Many Medicare Advantage plans offer a discount hearing benefit where you can get a no-cost hearing test within a network of hearing specialists. And you'll pay a set cost for hearing aids every few years—something similar to a $699 copay or $999 copay from an in-network provider such as TruHearing. Out-of-network you'll pay full cost.

Deciding to get coverage or not is more challenging for hearing aids as it depends on the level of hearing loss you have. And how quickly your hearing loss worsens over time. It's another task to work out as you make the transition to retirement. Put pencil to paper to figure out the best option for you individually.

Can you continue employer coverage in retirement?
Some employers allow their retired employees access to the dental, vision, and/or hearing benefits offered to workers. You may have such an option. Generally, you'll pay the full premium to remain in the plan, not the discounted premium you paid as an active employee. But this may be a good transition option.

Check your benefits information and talk to your HR or benefits team. And don't be disappointed if this is not an offer to retirees. Employers have no obligation to offer benefits to retirees. It's just something that may be an option in your case.

Last thoughts
Whether you choose to add one or more of these optional ingredients to your Medicare recipe is completely up to you, your health situation, and your budget. While the cost-sharing isn't great relative to the costs of major dental, many pairs of eyeglasses, and hearing aids, it is your money. You may want an extra $100 or $1,000 in your pocket.

Remember to assess the cost-benefit. Is paying $600/year worth it for $400 worth of cleanings at the dentist? But what if you need a crown in five years? It's a bit of a gamble for some.

It's important to check out today's options and keep shopping throughout retirement. There are many changes and new entrants in the market every year. And who knows, maybe the next Congress will expand Medicare to include some coverage.

You can use Health Savings Account (HSA) dollars to cover most if not all of these optional healthcare costs. If you have a Roth IRA, you might use some tax-free dollars to cover some expenses. Or simply set aside a bucket of money or earmark a particular account for healthcare costs in retirement. We are all responsible for our healthcare costs in retirement. The challenge is to find the right insurance or plans to help us pay for what we need.

CHAPTER 14

Important Information for Creating Your Medicare Recipe

Remember how frustrating it was when your third grader told you—just as he was going to bed—he needed to bring cookies to the bake sale? Tomorrow. Definitely an unwelcome late-night task ahead for you. You worked hard to whip up the best chocolate chip cookies for the little cherub. At 10 p.m. So frustrating!

Same concept goes for those reaching age 65 and it just dawns on them that perhaps they should explore this Medicare thing. They've heard something about Medicare and probably need to get some information. Their friends, siblings, and co-workers are all offering advice in loud and confident ways. And hundreds of mailers arrive from every insurance company known to mankind.

You hear yourself saying one morning, "I guess I'll take a peek…"

When to get started exploring this "Medicare" thing
Ideally, on your 60th birthday. And if you missed that opportunity, go with 62. Even taking a peek in the oven at 63 or 64 will save you some headaches. Whatever you do, do not wait until you are approaching your 65th birthday. Now you've landed in quicksand and you're going to regret not getting started sooner.

Why start so early? After all, the gates to Medicare only open the month containing your 65th birthday month. Five years in advance seems a bit premature, no? Frankly, the reason is to ease the shock. The system is wildly complex and getting things wrong will cost you more. Most people believe Medicare is free. Or at least, they expect to have significant savings on healthcare once they get into Medicare.

They could not be more wrong. Many people will see significantly higher healthcare costs in retirement than they imagined. Especially high-income and high-asset folks. Your personal costs are determined by your financial situation and the zip code and county you live in. Your personal health profile is a significant factor in your Medicare costs along with others such as:

- Your income throughout retirement.
- The plans offered in your area.
- The prescription drugs you are taking.
- Whether you are managing an expensive chronic condition or a rare health condition.
- If you are eligible for other alternatives to Medigap.
- If you have multiple homes, or spend considerable time outside of your zip code.

And so forth. No one can tell you if you should budget $400/month or $1,000/month. It's up to you to figure this out. The initial exploration you do well before age 65 will help you make key decisions about both Medicare and other health insurance options before 65. And budget accordingly.

In addition, understanding how Medicare pricing is determined will help you and your financial advisor make better strategic decisions, especially around deferred compensation, stock option settlements, and Roth conversions. Most people have no idea their Medicare Part B premium will be based on Modified Adjusted Gross Income (MAGI) two years in arrears. If you had a major income opportunity at age 63, plan to retire at 65, and start Medicare, or must start Part B because you work in a small business (fewer than 20 employees), you are going to be very unhappy that your Part B premium is not the standard rate. Rather, it tops $700 per month per person. For a married couple both on Medicare, that's up to $16,800 for one year of retirement. Plan accordingly.

While you won't go broke paying this rate, you may be upset and unhappy. It's bad enough to pay a premium where you only get a 25% subsidy from the federal government. But had you known back at age 60 this was heading your way, you would be prepared, would have budgeted properly, and may have made different decisions about when to sell stock, do a Roth conversion, or decide to retire.

You want the widest range of choices available to you when it comes to healthcare and health insurance costs in retirement. Being blind-sided is not helpful.

How should you evaluate your options?
As mentioned in previous chapters, you will find moving from group health plans offered by your employer to the individual market to be somewhat shocking. It's as if a brick wall was built at age 65. There are insurance rules for those under 65 and a different set for those 65 and older.

Learning about your options and evaluating the many plans and insurance companies will be important. It's a tall order and needs more than weekend. If you have waited too long, you may make a decision you're not happy with. Or you'll just go with what your cousin Nan selected or the plan your friend Julie picked. After all, they're really happy with their plans. But what if their plans don't cover all your healthcare needs? Then you're in a real jam.

Evaluating your options is not hard once you dive into the tools available on Medicare.gov. They are powerful, comprehensive tools. All insurers that participate in the Medicare market must provide Medicare with their plan details each year.

As of this publication, the Medicare website prominently displays the "find plans" tool on the homepage. Anyone and everyone can use the tool to shop for plans and prices. You'll simply click on the link to get into the tool, then choose to use the tool without logging in. You will not be able to save your results in the tool until you create an account. But to create a "MyMedicare" account, you need to be enrolled in either Part A or Part B and have your Medicare number.

However, you can "print to PDF" or print to paper. There is a tremendous amount of detail in every report, so printing is a wise idea. Especially when you are just getting started.

Evaluating Medigap plans
The steps you'll take to evaluate Medigap policies include:

- Entering your zip code and county of your legal residence.
- Answering any questions in the tool such as do you need "extra help" programs or not.
- Selecting that you want to review Medigap policies.

The output shows all the plans offered and available in your area. In 47 States, you'll see policies labeled with capital letters: A, B, D, G, K, L, M, and N. You'll see a summary of benefits covered in each plan, the range of monthly premiums, and a button to review specific plans.

In Massachusetts, Minnesota, and Wisconsin, you'll see different, more streamlined Medigap options. You'll also see cost information and a button to see the individual insurers offering plans in your zip code.

Important Information for Creating Your Medicare Recipe

Start pushing buttons. You want to get to the list of insurers offering the policy you are interested in.

The most important things to remember about shopping for Medigap policies are:

- Choose the specific benefits you want covered—from basic coverage to full coverage.
- Check the price of the policy. Remember, all Medigaps in the same letter must cover the same benefits. Don't pay more for the same coverage.
- Assess the credibility and rating of the insurance company. If you've never heard of a company, you probably don't want to give them your money.

Create a comparison chart to evaluate different options. Over the next couple of years, go back to take a fresh look at the insurers and how they've changed pricing. It is a fascinating exercise.

Evaluating standalone Part D plans

When looking at drug plans, the key is finding the lowest cost plan that covers all your Rx's. But do not be fooled by just looking at the topline summary page. The hidden part of Part D plans is that the insurers are in cahoots with the pharmacies. You'll see the lowest priced plan when you first run your numbers. But you'll only get that if you choose the right pharmacy.

You enter the find plans tool the same way. On Medicare.GOV (not Medicare.com), put in your zip code and county. Answer any questions, then select Part D plans. You'll be asked to enter your prescriptions. Put them in exactly as your prescription is written. Line up your pill bottles and other Rx's and enter the information on the labels.

When you're finished adding drugs, continue on to choose pharmacies—mail order and four other local stores. Usually, you want to check brand name pharmacies first. You can change the pharmacies later. But start with your best guess and look at the results.

You are looking for the cheapest Part D plan that covers all your drugs. It is that simple. These plans are only one-year contracts so get the best option in your zip code for this year. You will reshop your Part D plan every year in retirement between October 15 and December 7. Once your choose your new plan, it will start on January 1st.

Special note: Expect a lot of price changes—both good and bad—in Part D plan premiums and costs of drugs over the next several years as the Inflation Reduction Act gets implemented. With a $2,000 cap on out-of-pocket covered drug costs for those on Medicare, I would not be surprised to see steeper increases in monthly premiums each year. Or in the retail costs of some prescriptions. Keep a close watch on prices.

Evaluating Medicare Advantage with drug plans
This is a trying exercise at best. There is truly nothing easy about finding the best MAPD that meets your healthcare needs. You might find three well-known insurance companies to consider, dig through their websites, read the plan documents, and get familiar with the various options. Most insurance companies don't offer just one MAPD. Instead, they offer multiple HMOs and PPOs, each with a different drug plan.

It is up to you to build your own comparison chart to see what the various plans offer. Then, lay out several health scenarios and use their plan documents to try to estimate your copays and other OOP costs. And, finally, determine if the Rx's you take are covered by each plan.

An important step is to contact the physicians you must continue to see. It's up to you to ask them (or try checking the databases on each insurer's website) if they are in the network for the MAPD you are considering. They don't have to be in the network. If that is the case, you might spend more to get a PPO where you'll pay higher copays to use out-of-network physicians and services. Or find a new physician who accepts the plan you want.

The MAPD you choose is only a one-year plan. You are responsible for reshopping your MAPD each year during Open Enrollment Period: October 15 – December 7. And it's critically important to check with your doctors and hospital systems if they are accepting the plan you want each following year.

MAPDs may be helpful in coordinating your care. But if you go this route, you are choosing to be heavily involved in the gamesmanship of insurance companies and hospital systems throughout your retirement. Consider the factors in Table 13 (next page) when deciding which avenue to go.

Table 13. Comparison of key factors between Medigap and MAPD, 2025

	Medigap	Part C/HMO	Part C/PPO
Monthly Premium	Higher, but steady Premiums	Lower Premiums, even $0	Lower Premiums, even $0
Choice of Physicians	High Flexibility	Low Flexibility	Higher flexibility, higher cost
Choice of Specialists	High Flexibility	Low Flexibility	Higher flexibility, higher cost
Choice of Hospitals/Clinics	YES	Generally, NO	YES, but higher cost Out-of-network
Referrals Required	NO	Generally, YES	NO
Self-advocating in some situations	NO	YES	YES
SNF requires in-network	NO	Generally, YES	Generally, YES
Risk paying more for SNF	NO	YES	YES
Level of involvement in plan details	Very Low	Medium	High
Your Location	National Options	Generally, local area	Wider regional range
Filing a Claim	Handled via your doctor	Out-of-network issues	Out-of-network issues
OOP "nickel & dime" costs	NO	YES	YES
Annual OOP	Monthly premium x 12	High max: $3,400 - $9,350	High max: $5,000 - $14,000
Plan can be canceled	Generally, NO	YES, notified by Sept	YES, notified by Sept
Doctor/groups can stop taking plan	NO	YES	YES

(SNF is a Skilled Nursing Facility. OOP is out-of-pocket.)

Should spouses buy the same plan at the same insurer?
No. That's the simple answer. There is no reason for spouses to have the same Medicare recipe. Each individual needs to select the ingredients that work best for them and their health profile. Sometimes, insurers offer limited discounts if spouses buy the same plan, but don't let that influence your decision. The discounts are short-lived, lasting only two or three years.

That being said, in reality most couples choose the same general strategy. They both choose Original Medicare A and B plus the same Medigap Plan G. Or they both choose the same MAPD insurer.

Where things tend to be different is with Part D plans. Because each person takes different prescriptions—or one spouse takes Rx's and the other doesn't—typically each spouse finds a different Part D plan that is the least expensive for their basket of prescriptions.

Part D plans have a one-year shelf life. It may be that the spouses have Part D plans from two different insurers for the first five years. Then in year six, because so much changes opaquely behind the scenes, they both end up with the same Part D plan. It's always a surprise.

Can't I switch from MAPD to Medigap like the commercials indicate?

No. Not usually. Well, maybe. It depends.

You can switch MAPDs. And you can switch from Original Medicare with a Medigap to a MAPD. The problem is when you want to drop your MAPD and get into Original Medicare, you often cannot buy a Medigap. Unless you live in MA, CT, ME, or NY or in a few other states like Illinois that allow limited changes at certain ages, insurers do not have to sell you a Medigap in most situations.

In general, you want to think of making your Medicare decision as a 30-year decision. You either go the Medigap route, or the Part C route. The two do not mix, and it's not often that you can switch lanes.

In the opinion of many of us who spend an inordinate amount of time in Medicare land, we think most of the commercials on TV and in the media are terribly misleading. They are technically correct…in that they aren't telling you anything wrong. But the information provided is far from complete.

The key to deciding if you want to be in the MAPD lane is reading all the fine print. All 200 pages in the plan documents before you decide. Know before you buy.

So why can't you switch from a MAPD to a Medigap? Usually it's because you are older and sicker. That's when most folks figure out their MAPD isn't very flexible. And they are stuck in a network. But now they are 80 and need other care. Or their care plan has been denied by the MAPD. But they haven't paid into a Medigap plan for the past 15 years, essentially pre-paying for future services. The insurance company isn't going to allow them to just come in the door when they will be a high-user of healthcare dollars.

You can try to switch from MAPD to Medigap. It requires phone calls, undergoing medical underwriting—where the insurer will ask you a battery of personal health questions and dig into your health records—and assessing the cost. You may be able to get into a Medigap plan, but the insurer can and generally will charge you a higher monthly premium. And you may need to wait six months before your condition is insurable.

It's important to think like an insurance company. You first need to keep your profits up. And you have to pay for hundreds of thousands of people's care. It's unfair for a sick person to all of a sudden show up. They won't be paying premiums for 30 years and now need costs covered. That's not how the business of insurance works.

CREATING YOUR MEDICARE RECIPE

CHAPTER 15

Where to Get Expert Help

If you watch food shows on TV or online, you get many tips for making better chocolate chip cookies from chefs and bakers. You might find yourself baking better in your own kitchen.

When it comes to selecting Medicare options, using experts can be helpful. There are resources that won't cost you anything, and others that will. Recommendations from friends and family can help you get started, but what works for them may not work for you.

Every state has S.H.I.P. representatives
Creating your best Medicare recipe can be complicated. The SHIP organization—State Health Insurance (Assistance) Program—is available at no cost to everyone. You can meet with a volunteer in your zip code who can help you navigate options and choose the parts and pieces that work for your personal situation.

The SHIP folks are particularly helpful if you have a difficult situation such as a high-cost drug you can't find coverage for, a parent who has run out of money, or finding a better plan to meet a new healthcare need.

These helpers are often located in your local Senior Center, or you can find them at your public library. Check the website for more information: https://www.shiphelp.org/

Helpful hint: SHIP representatives are very busy during annual Open Enrollment Period, October 15 – December 7. Try to meet with them outside this time to do your planning.

Find an independent, unbiased fee-only person
The mainstay of the insurance industry is using brokers or agents who are paid a commission to sell you an insurance product. But there is another option. You can search for a fee-only, independent person or company to help you navigate Medicare and create your recipe.

These folks are harder to find but are out there. I do many Medicare fee-only consultations for an hourly rate, and I like the team at i65 Medicare. Most fee-only businesses help financial advisors and individuals. Your own financial advisor should have someone on their team to support the complex Medicare decisions as should your accountant. The special value they bring to your party is assessing *all* insurance options available in your zip code. They aren't cherry-picking and selling you only the few plans they get paid on.

That said, there are some excellent brokers and agents out there...

If you use a broker or agent, what should you ask them?
There are thousands of insurance brokers and agents who help people sign up for Medicare. They make a good living. But due to the nature of this unwieldy beast called health insurance, there are some conflicts when selling insurance. For one, brokers and agents do not sell all options available to you. Typically, they have three to six companies on their platform. The option they present to you may be the right one. But maybe it's not. How will you know?

The bigger concern is how the brokers and agents get paid. There's no issue that they get paid on commission. Lots of hard workers get paid on commission. The issue is they get paid two to three times more for selling you a Medicare Advantage plan than a Medigap plan. And that builds in bias to the process.

As of 2025, Congress is starting to address some of these egregious commission schemes. Every year in the Federal Register, CMS and the federal government set the commission rates for MAPDs. For 2025, the national average broker commission rate is $626 per MAPD sold, and $313 for each plan that renews. Brokers in certain high-costs states get higher commissions.[16]

But there is no set standard for selling Medigap plans. Typically, the insurer pays brokers a percentage of the annual premium. If a Medigap Plan G has a $2,640 annual premium, the broker might receive between $275 and $450 to sell this plan. But someone buying Plan G high-deductible at $80/month results in a commission of approximately $100 to $200. The agent will also get a much smaller renewal fee when you remain in the Medigap plan, and only for a few years.

Part D plans add a little extra at $100 per plan sold. But even when combined with a Medigap plan, a broker clearly doubles the commission by selling one MAPD.

Needless to say, there is a gigantic incentive for agents and brokers to sell you a MAPD and lock you into a network. Buyer beware!

Top 13 questions to ask a broker or agent – a baker's dozen
It's critical you ask the right questions when working with an agent or broker. Here's my list of top 13 questions you should ask before doing business with an insurance broker or agent:

1. How many plans are offered in my zip code? How many of those plans do you sell?
2. Do you only sell one company's insurance plans? (Someone who works for Blue Cross, for example, can only sell that one company's products.)

3. How much commission do you get paid if I buy a MAPD from you?
4. How much commission do you receive if I buy a Medigap and Part D?
5. Do you get paid next year if I don't make any changes to my plan? If so, how much and for how long?
6. If I run into a problem with the MAPD plan denying or delaying my care, do you help with the appeals process?
7. If my plan charges more than I expected, do you help me figure out my bill?
8. If my prescriptions change mid-year, can you help me find a new plan or find an interim solution until the Open Enrollment Period?
9. If I want to switch later from a MAPD to a Medigap, will you help me find a good option?
10. If I want to start with a MAPD but switch to a Medigap in a few years, how easy will it be to do so? Tell me about your clients who have tried this switch. Were they allowed into a Medigap? Did they have to pay more?
11. Can you explain the differences between an HMO, PPO, and PPFS? Why should I chose the one you are recommending? How much more will it cost me if I go out-of-network?
12. What if the hospital I go to pulls out of the MAPD you've recommended when I'm 80?
13. Do you have a broker/agent check or references I can review to see if you are a professional in good standing?

Last note about pricing and commissions. Some independent agencies have very helpful representatives you can work with.

And their websites are chock-full of good information. The agents will tell you they get paid a salary...and that is often the case. However, the company itself gets paid more when their employees sell a MAPD instead of a Medigap. Insurance companies get significantly higher revenues from the federal government on every Medicare beneficiary who buys a MAPD. And their profits soar on the backs of those individuals using the networks in MAPDs.

It's always about the money. Your health insurance is no different.

CREATING YOUR MEDICARE RECIPE

CHAPTER 16

Resources and a Worksheet to Create Your Medicare Recipe

You are now at the point where you can mix all your ingredients together and get your cookies in the oven. You are ready to create your own Medicare recipe.

To help you along, let me show you an example. Think of this as trying a sample as you walk through the grocery store.

Pulling together your Medicare recipe
In the example, you'll see each of the Medicare ingredients on one side of the table, including some placeholder costs for drugs. You will ultimately choose either a Medigap plan with a standalone Part D plan as shown, or a MAPD. While the MAPD monthly premium may be $0, you must also build in your estimated copays, coinsurance charges, and out-of-network costs, plus estimated drug costs. You typically pay separately for your Rx's even in a MAPD.

Using 2024 as the base year, you can see how costs might increase. I use a flat 5% inflation rate and apply it to all pieces and parts. This gives you a general direction of how costs could increase throughout retirement.

On the other side of the table, you'll see other optional ingredients you may need to build into your recipe. How you solve for dental, vision, and hearing will be based on your own research

CREATING YOUR MEDICARE RECIPE

and preferences. If you pay a premium for a plan, the out-of-pocket costs for services should be lower. If you decide to pay on your own, build in your own best estimates. For dental, I used a premium-based plan. For vision and hearing, I skipped buying a plan and assumed out-of-pocket costs instead.

In the end, you must decide what works for you. If you are married or have a partner, make sure to lay out the options and costs for each of you. Every individual gets to create their own Medicare recipe.

A Medicare and retirement healthcare cost example

Table 14. Example of annual costs for a full "Medicare" recipe. Your own costs will be different.

Medicare Components H/C est. inflation = 1.05

ESTIMATES Per MONTH	2024 Costs	2025 Costs	2026 Est Costs	2027 Est Costs	2028 Est Costs
Medicare Part A	$0	$0	$0	$0	$0
Medicare Part B	$174.70	$185	$194	$204	$214
Part B IRMAA	$0	$0	$0	$0	$0
Medigap	$200	$210	$221	$232	$243
Part C Premium (if applicable)	$0	$0	$0	$0	$0
Part C Copays (if applicable)	$0	$0	$0	$0	$0
Part D premium	$15	$16	$17	$17	$18
Part D IRMAA	$0	$0	$0	$0	$0
Est cost of Rx's	$25	$26	$28	$29	$30
TOTAL Monthly Cost	$415	$437	$459	$482	$506
TOTAL Annual Cost	$4,976	$5,244	$5,506	$5,782	$6,071

Other health costs expected in retirement

Other Health Costs Expected in Retirement   H/C est. inflation = 1.05

ESTIMATES per YEAR	2024 Est Costs	2025 Est Costs	2026 Est Costs	2027 Est Costs	2028 Est Costs
Dental Plan: cost or premium	$600	$630	$662	$695	$729
Dental - basic	$100	$105	$110	$116	$122
Dental - major	$0	$0	$0	$1,500	$0
Vision Plan: cost or premium	$0	$0	$0	$0	$0
Vision - exams	$150	$158	$165	$174	$182
Vision - glasses, contacts	$1,200	$0	$1,260	$0	$1,323
Hearing - exams	$0	$275	$0	$0	$300
Hearing aids	$0	$7,500	$0	$0	$7,875
Podiatry services, non-covered	$0	$0	$0	$0	$0
OTC drugs	$100	$105	$110	$116	$122
OTC other - first aid	$100	$105	$110	$116	$122
OTC other - comfort	$150	$158	$165	$174	$182
TOTAL Annual Cost	$2,400	$9,035	$2,583	$2,889	$10,957
Total Monthly Cost	$200	$753	$215	$241	$913
Grand Total Monthly Costs	$615	$1,190	$674	$723	$1,419
Grand Total Annual Costs	$7,376	$14,279	$8,089	$8,671	$17,027

CREATING YOUR MEDICARE RECIPE

A blank template for you to create your Medicare recipe and estimated costs

Medicare Components   H/C est. inflation = 1.05

ESTIMATES per MONTH	2025 Est Costs	2026 Est Costs	2027 Est Costs	2028 Est Costs	2029 Est Costs
Medicare Part A					
Medicare Part B					
Part B IRMAA					
Medigap					
Part C Premium (if applicable)					
Part C Copays (if applicable)					
Part D premium					
Part D IRMAA					
Est cost of Rx's					
TOTAL Monthly Cost					
TOTAL Annual Cost					

Other Health Costs Expected in Retirement   H/C est. inflation = 1.05

ESTIMATES Per YEAR	2025 Est Costs	2026 Est Costs	2027 Est Costs	2028 Est Costs	2029 Est Costs
Dental Plan: cost or premium					
Dental - basic					
Dental - major					
Vision Plan: cost or premium					
Vision - exams					
Vision - glasses, contacts					
Hearing - exams					
Hearing aids					
Podiatry services, non-covered					
OTC drugs					
OTC other - first aid					
OTC other - comfort					
TOTAL Annual Cost					
TOTAL Monthly Cost					
Grand Total Monthly Costs					
Grand Total Annual Costs					

Medicare resources and more

Handy resources to help build your Medicare recipe:

Medicare.gov – Use the tools on the official Medicare website. (Do not use Medicare.com—this is a private company website and does not provide all options available.)

Medicare & You – This book is provided by Medicare and updated annually. You can request a copy or download it at https://www.medicare.gov/basics/forms-publications-mailings/mailings/other/medicare-you-handbook

SSA.gov – The Social Security website where you apply for Medicare Part A and Part B. And Social Security when you are ready to claim benefits.

CMS.gov – Centers for Medicare and Medicaid Services website.

Boomer Retirement Briefs – My long-running blog chocked full of Social Security and Medicare posts near-retirees need to know about. https://boomerretirementbriefs.com/

AARP.org – They have a Medicare section with questions and answers. Very helpful.

RetirementDaily.net – A daily newsletter covering Medicare and Social Security topics.

KFF.org – An unbiased and independent source for health policy research, polling, and news.

Other books by Marcia MacDonald Mantell

Cookin' Up Your Retirement Plan – This is a discussion guide with a variety of worksheets you can use as you plan your move into retirement.

What's the Deal with Social Security for Women – Here you'll find background, rules, and clear examples of how Social Security applies in different situations. Equally important for men to read.

What's the Deal with Retirement Planning for Women – This book asks 13 key questions you should answer before you retire. There's no point in missing key ingredients here either.

Endnotes

1 Social Security Administration. https://www.ssa.gov/history/1939amends.html#:~:text=This%20change%20transformed%20Social%20Security,became%20a%20pivotal%20turning%2Dpoint.

2 National Archives, Harry S. Truman Library. https://www.trumanlibrary.gov/education/presidential-inquiries/challenge-national-healthcare

3 KFF, Medicare Advantage in 2024: Premiums, Out-of-Pocket Limits, Supplemental Benefits, and Prior Authorization. Meredith Freed, Jeannie Fuglesten Biniek, Anthony Damico, and Tricia Neuman

Published: Aug 08, 2024   https://www.kff.org/medicare/issue-brief/medicare-advantage-in-2024-premiums-out-of-pocket-limits-supplemental-benefits-and-prior-authorization/#:~:text=In%20contrast%2C%20traditional%20Medicare%20does,%2Dof%2Dnetwork%20services%20combined

4 Medicare.gov and CMS. Costs for 2024 https://www.cms.gov/newsroom/fact-sheets/2024-medicare-parts-b-premiums-and-deductibles

5 Ibid.

6 Medigap.com Average Cost of Medigap Insurance Plans, October 05, 2023. Lindsay Malzone   https://www.medigap.com/faqs/average-cost-of-medigap-insurance-plans/#:~:text=Medigap%20policy%20premium.-,Issue%2Dage%2Drated%20policies,his%20monthly%20premium%20is%20$185.

Endnotes

7 Medicare.gov and CMS. Costs for 2024 https://www.medicare.gov/drug-coverage-part-d/costs-for-medicare-drug-coverage/yearly-deductible-for-drug-plans#:~:text=This%20is%20the%20amount%20you,more%20than%20$545%20in%202024.

8 See endnote 3.

9 2024 Annual Report of The Boards of Trustees of the Federal Hospital Insurance and Federal Supplementary Medical Insurance Trust Funds, Table V.E1. HI Cost-Sharing and premium Amounts https://www.cms.gov/oact/tr/2024

10 Medicare Part B: Enrollment and Premiums, Congressional Research Service, Updated June 15, 2021, and 2024 Annual Report Of The Boards Of Trustees of the Federal Hospital Insurance and Federal Supplementary Medical Insurance Trust Funds.

11 CMS.gov, Original Medicare Eligibility and Enrollment, https://www.cms.gov/medicare/enrollment-renewal/original-part-a-b#:~:text=Be%20a%20U.S.%20resident;%20AND,filing%20an%20application%20for%20Medicare.

12 See endnote 9.

13 KFF, Data Note: Prescription Drugs and Older Adults. Ashley Kirzinger, Tricia Neuman, Juliette Cubanski, and Mollyann Brodie. Published: Aug 09, 2019. https://www.kff.org/affordable-care-act/issue-brief/data-note-prescription-drugs-and-older-adults/

14 CMS, The Balanced Budget Act of 1997 (BBA) established a new Part C of the Medicare program, known then as the Medicare+Choice (M+C) program, effective January 1999. https://www.cms.gov/medicare/enrollment-renewal/health-plans#:~:text=The%20Balanced%20Budget%20Act%20of,)%20program%2C%20effective%20January%201999.

15 Nursing Home Costs and Payment Options, Kate Van Dis, Sept 16, 2024, based on Genworth's 2023 survey of nursing home prices. https://www.ncoa.org/adviser/local-care/nursing-homes-costs/

16 Medicare Drug & Health Plan Contract Administration Group, July 2024, https://go.actionbenefits.com/hubfs/Memo_Updated_AB_Compensation_and_T_and_Testing_Requirements_CY2025_Final.pdf

www.ingramcontent.com/pod-product-compliance
Lightning Source LLC
Chambersburg PA
CBHW060503030426
42337CB00015B/1716